FOSTER FAMILIES FOR ADULTS

Columbia Studies of Social Gerontology and Aging

Columbia Studies of Social Gerontology and Aging
Abraham Monk, *General Editor*

FOSTER FAMILIES FOR ADULTS

A Community Alternative in Long-Term Care

Susan R. Sherman
Evelyn S. Newman

Columbia University Press
New York   1988

Columbia University Press
New York   Guildford, Surrey
Copyright © 1988 Columbia University Press
Printed in the United States of America

Library of Congress Cataloging-in-Publication Data

Sherman, Susan (Susan R.)
  Foster families for adults: a community alternative in long-term care/Susan R. Sherman, Evelyn S. Newman.
      p.   cm. — (Columbia studies of social gerontology and aging)
  Bibliography: p.
  Includes index.
  ISBN (invalid) 0-231-06086-0
  1. Aged—Home care—United States.   2. Foster home care—United States.   I. Newman, Evelyn S.   II. Title.   III. Series.
HV1461.S525 1988
362.6'3—dc 19

Hardback editions of Columbia University Press books are Smyth-sewn and are printed on permanent and durable acid-free paper.

In honor of Louise and Lester Roth and Joseph and Esther Zatlin, who first showed us the meaning of family, and to the memory of David S. Roth who enriched the family immeasurably.

Contents

Tables

Preface

It is increasingly recognized that the diversity of elderly persons requires a diversity of living arrangements. One option that has been used for both the frail elderly and those with psychiatric or developmental disabilities is foster family care. Foster care as a social intervention measure for children has been given a great deal of attention and scrutiny. However, much less is known about this option for adults. Despite a long history, this option has not been sufficiently explored for the frail elderly who do not need institutionalization, but who do require some support if they are to remain in the community. This book explores foster family care as one option within a continuum of sheltered housing for adults and focuses specifically on the integration of the resident into the host family and into the larger community. We shall also examine the roles of the various actors in this setting, including the resident, the foster family, and agency personnel.

In 1964 a statement in *Aging*, the official publication of the U.S. Department of Health, Education, and Welfare, claimed that "adult foster home care, one of the newer programs for older people, has been catching on. And with good reason. For in communities throughout the country, there are more and more older people who are too frail to live alone but not so ill or mentally impaired they

need to enter an institution" (USDHEW 1964:1). It is our contention that two points of that statement deserve comment.

First, we must point out that although adult foster home care
specifically for the elderly is a relatively recent development, the
practice of opening one's home to unrelated, dependent adults has
been in operation for centuries in Europe. In this country, Massachusetts officially began to operate a foster family care program
for mentally ill adults in 1885 (Morrissey 1967). Second, we question the extent to which the program "has been catching on." We
found it interesting, for example, that although the 1965 edition of
the *Encyclopedia of Social Work* contained a fairly detailed section
on "Foster and Home Care for Adults," neither the 1977 edition
nor the 1983–84 supplement contained a similar section—indicating a certain degree of neglect at least on the part of the social
work community and perhaps on the part of other professionals as
well.[1] In the 1987 edition Oktay commented that "although the
number of adult foster care programs has tripled since 1960, they
remain relatively unknown, and they are unavailable in many parts
of the United States" (1987:635).

In the 1965 *Encyclopedia* article Aptekar claimed: "The most basic problem in this type of social service program appears to be one
of interpretation to both the lay and the social work community"
(1965:355). It is our hope that this book will contribute to such an
"interpretation." The data in the book are from three studies of
foster family care for adults in New York State. The populations
included those in the social services system, those in the mental
hygiene system, and those in the mental retardation system. Because we are primarily interested in the psychosocial issues of family and community integration for these populations, rather than the
operation of the specific agencies, we believe the study has gen-
eralizability to other states and other program auspices.

Our definition of adult foster care includes what has been referred to both as family care and as foster care. The two terms

---

1. In 1977 foster homes were mentioned briefly in sections on aging: long-term
care institutions (Brody 1977); institutions for adults (Sherwood 1977); and protective services for adults (Follett 1977). In 1983–84 foster or family care homes were
mentioned briefly in a section on deinstitutionalization (Segal and Baumohl 1983).

represent two different historical origins: the care of the mentally ill and the care of the poor elderly without families. At present, both these categories of care include the salient features of a private family home, taking in a small number of nonrelated individuals, and offering some form of support. Placement and ongoing supervision are provided by a public or private agency.

The agencies placing residents in foster family care emphasize participation in the life of the family as an element distinguishing this setting from institutional care (State of New York, Department of Social Services 1971). Dictionary definitions of foster care include the notions of promoting growth, encouraging development, and providing nurturance. In the case of adults, it is important, we believe, that this nurturing environment be age-appropriate without infantilizing the residents. We agree with Provencal and Mac-Cormack that "highly desirable environments can be created for adult clients from a combination of carefully selected age-appropriate elements of foster care as well as other habilitative concepts" (1979:4). In many instances, there is a need for the environments to be not merely custodial but therapeutic as well.

It is our contention that a properly run adult foster care program can offer therapeutic care for all three dependent populations: the frail elderly, the mentally ill, and the mentally retarded/developmentally disabled. Very often the three groups overlap, and we find that the residents of foster family care for the mentally ill or mentally retarded tend to be older than their proportion of the various populations would indicate. Cotten, Sison, and Starr (1981), Di-Giovanni (1978), and Janicki and MacEachron (1984) have commented specifically on the elderly as a rapidly growing segment of the population of persons who are mentally retarded. Although there is growing awareness of the fact that persons with mental retardation who are elderly have special needs, there is little research on the most appropriate services for this group.

Foster family care may be used both as a postinstitutional placement or to prevent or delay institutionalization. Increasingly there is a recognition that with adequate community support, many disabled or elderly persons may be kept out of institutions. Foster care has been considered particularly appropriate for deinstitutionalized adults with the following characteristics: "advanced age . . . com-

plex medical or developmental problems . . . multiple handicaps"
(Provencal and MacCormack 1979:4) no suitable home conditions,
and rejection by their family (Maletz 1942). It is well known that
persons without families have an increased risk of institutionalization. It is also questionable whether family members are capable of
caring for deinstitutionalized older relatives in a sustained manner,
particularly whether they are able to "provide a therapeutic environment" (Maddox 1975:342). It may be that artificially created families with consequently less emotional involvement can tolerate difficult behavior to a greater extent than can the "natural" family.
Similarly, limited economic and social resources, both of which may
be particularly problematic for the very old, are associated with the
risk of institutionalization. This higher risk coupled with an aversion
toward institutionalization offers, we believe, a good argument for
placing older adults in foster families when they have no families
of their own who can provide care.

Over the years concern for and the philosophy of care for those
in need have gone through many changes. The uneven development of community as opposed to institutional care for dependent
groups is discussed in chapter 1. The chapter details how dependent persons have been cared for (or neglected) over time and describes the development and changing philosophy of foster care for
adults. Chapter 1 also introduces the constructs important to our
analysis.

In our research we have studied three populations for whom foster family care represents a useful option. These populations are
described in further detail in the second chapter: the frail elderly
and middle-aged and older mentally ill and mentally retarded persons. We have interviewed both providers and residents, and have
used departmental records as well. Our methodology is described
in chapter 2.

The literature regarding adult foster care tends to be sparse and
tends to emphasize the financial advantages of family care, rather
than the quality or outcome of care. Intagliata, Willer, and Wicks
(1981) have commented that the many studies of community adjustment of formerly institutionalized mentally retarded persons tend
to use a single criterion of success, namely, recidivism. Little attention is paid to the quality of adjustment. We extend the liter-

ature by focusing upon the psychosocial issues of integration into the family and integration into the community. In questioning the desirability of foster care, Herz (1971) concluded that foster family care does not really provide a "family" atmosphere but instead becomes an agency-supervised boarding home. Chapter 3 examines indicators of familism and the extent to which integration into the life of the family occurs. We also discuss an unanticipated positive outcome found in many of the foster families. Quite often the only "family" until the arrival of the new placement was a single individual. Only with the arrival of the new member was a true family created, thus bringing companionship and nurture to both the home owner and the foster family member.

Janicki's definition of integration includes the use of community services, encouragement to become members of the greater community, and prevention of the community's view of the residents as merely "transient consumers" (1981:63). Chapter 4 explores the extent to which the clients are integrated into the life of the community. We are interested in both acceptance by the community and participation in the community. We also examine the characteristics of providers, residents, and home that are associated with enhanced community integration.

Chapter 5 discusses the roles of the foster family, the resident, the social worker, and the "natural family." The literature on adult foster care contains few systematic analyses of the interaction between resident, caseworker, and care provider (Linn and Caffey 1977; Miller 1977; Watt 1970). Therefore, in our study we focus on this interaction during each part of the process of adult foster care: recruitment and training of the provider, selection and placement of the client, as well as supervision and follow-up. We offer some suggestions for increasing the response to the program.

We are witnessing recent initiatives to stabilize and expand foster family care. Given the increase in the very old population and the increasing necessity for long-term care, coupled with dissatisfaction with current service options, it is timely to examine foster care as an option that can be used efficiently and humanely. Our book provides an in-depth examination of foster care as a service for adults at high risk. The data represent a unique opportunity in public policy analysis. Clients are included from three public systems; we consider the important policy question of community treatment of the impaired; and study comparatively a particular option—foster care, with its distinct opportunity for life within a family. We describe the roles of the various participants, with special attention to the transactions among all these parties. We offer recommendations for policy, training, support, and supervision. It is our hope that the information in this book will be useful to care providers and to agencies such as departments of aging, social services, mental health, and mental retardation, as well as to older persons and their families.

Acknowledgments

These studies were partially funded by a grant from the Aging Research Coordination Project of the State University of New York at Albany, supported by the New York State Office for the Aging under Title III of the Older Americans Act, and by two grants from the New York State Health Research Council, New York State Department of Health. We wish to thank David Sutton of the Office for the Aging and John Jack of the Health Research Council for their assistance in obtaining this support. The senior author was given the opportunity to work on the manuscript during a sabbatical leave from the State University of New York at Albany.

A study that has taken place over so many years has indebted us to many people. Most especially we wish to thank the care providers and residents who welcomed us into their homes and graciously shared their experience with us. We hope this book reflects their aspirations and accomplishments.

Two colleagues deserve special thanks. Eleanor Frenkel served as project coordinator for the second and third phases of our research. During that time she participated in every stage of the research endeavor, and contributed her insight and creativity to every task. We are greatly indebted to her. Edmund Sherman of the School of Social Welfare at the State University of New York at Albany consulted with us in the earliest stages of our research and writing. More recently, he has read the manuscript, and made numerous thoughtful suggestions. The entire book has benefited from his advice.

Many other colleagues have made contributions at various stages. We would particularly like to thank Jan Hagen, Malcolm Sherman, Sheldon Tobin, and Lynn Videka-Sherman. To others who have offered assistance and encouragement over the years, we extend our appreciation. We are also grateful to Abraham Monk and Louise Waller for their assistance throughout the editorial process.

We are indebted to numerous staff members of the agencies involved in adult foster family care. The study would not have been possible without the enormous contributions of staff of the New York State Department of Social Services, the New York State Office of Mental Health, the New York State Office of Mental Retardation and Developmental Disabilities, the New York State Board of Social Welfare, and the Albany Veterans Administration Hospital. Staff at both the state and local levels provided administrative information and assisted with sampling, access to providers, and questionnaire development. We especially would like to thank Cheryl Ashworth, Arthur Doring, John Greene, John Jacobson, Matthew Janicki, Milton Kaplan, Roy Minard, Tom O'Brien, and Shirley Thomas, who facilitated our field work. To all the other agency personnel who gave us assistance, we also extend our thanks.

Several research assistants helped with interviewing, coding, data processing, and analysis. They are Larry Brown, Susan Bubb, Dennis Chapman, Victoria Gambitsky, Claire Higgins, Nora Lynch, Bethany Newman, Gayle Pignone, Emily Stewart, Carolyn Teich, Donna Thomson, Deborah Traynor, Sarah Traynor, and John Wren. We are grateful for their interest and dedication.

Several typists at the School of Social Welfare assisted with the production of reports and survey instruments. Special acknowledgment is extended to Barbara Rogers, our secretary during most of this project. She worked tirelessly, enthusiastically, and most professionally.

Deepest love and gratitude are expressed to Malcolm, Barbara, and Michael Sherman, who always demonstrate the importance of family. This book, and the research on which it is based, have been sustained and enhanced by Mal's constant professional and personal wisdom and support. Sheldon Kaufman has been present when family could not be. He provided support and encouragement when it was most needed.

1 · History and Philosophy of Foster Family Care

Foster care is easily understood and accepted as a social intervention measure for children. Foster care for adults, however, is neither as readily accepted nor understood, despite the fact that foster home care was used for adults before it was used for children (McCoin 1983). "The practice of placing unrelated, dependent adults in the care of private families is the oldest known form of community care—indeed, the oldest form of social service in continuous use—in the world" (Bogen 1979:5). As a matter of fact, it may be noted that family care is the oldest form of community placement of the New York State Office of Mental Health (State of New York, OMH 1983:27).

Currently, in foster care it is expected that "the host family will maintain an interest in [the individual's] psychological, social, and physical well-being. . . . The family is assisted by a public or private agency, hospital, or institution that usually finds the family and assumes financial, casework, and other types of responsibility for the individual who is placed" (Aptekar 1965:351). The practice of providing care for adults without familial resources is an ancient one that has its origin in the legend of St. Dymphna.

According to legend, although incestuous marriages were common at the time, Princess Dymphna, in A.D. 600, was horrified by what she considered an "insane" proposal of marriage from her widowed father. She fled her home in Ireland and sailed for Europe. Her father overtook her near Gheel, Belgium, where he decapitated her and the priest traveling with her. In the belief that Dymphna's martyrdom represented a victory over the "devils" that made her father mad, her grave became a shrine that attracted similarly afflicted persons seeking relief from their own "devils," i.e., persons who were considered "spiritually ill" (Bogen 1979; McCoin 1983; Morrissey 1967). When the Catholic church became too small to house all the pilgrims who came to the shrine, the church placed with families in Gheel hundreds of mentally ill persons seeking cure. Records of family care provided for the mentally ill in Gheel go back as far as 1250 (Aptekar 1965). The sponsorship of the program in Gheel remained with the Catholic church until the government assumed control in 1852 (Bogen 1979; Morrissey 1967).

Before continuing the story of family care after its establishment in Gheel, we place family care in a more general historical context of institutional and community treatment for several frail and dependent populations. While foster homes were originally set up to serve the "insane," today such homes represent the confluence of three service streams, providing both custodial and rehabilitative services for the mentally ill, the mentally retarded/developmentally disabled, and the frail elderly. Although foster homes were used for the adult mentally ill for centuries, this model was not used extensively for the elderly until the 1940s (Aptekar 1965). Aptekar in 1965 was one of the first to refer to the use of foster care specifically for the elderly. Obviously, this reflects changing life expectancy, i.e., a need to provide support and care for some of the growing numbers of persons who survive into old age.

This book deals with foster care for the dependent older person, whether the person comes through the mental health system, the mental retardation system, or programs for the elderly. We discuss a system of care that has evolved on the one hand from family care and other options for the mentally ill, and on the other hand from boarding homes and almshouses for the poor elderly. After examining issues in the care of dependent adults, we return to the history of foster family care and to the forces that have led to resistance to this type of care.

CARE FOR THE DEPENDENT IN AMERICA

Care for the mentally ill, the mentally retarded, and the aged has not been a steady progression in a single direction. Over the centuries calls for reform have reflected both the philosophic and economic attitudes of their times. Such attitudes run the gamut from altruism to neglect or even punishment. Thus, depending upon the spirit of the time, persons in need have sometimes been regarded as requiring the largesse of society, but more often as deserving their condition for wasting their resources. With regard to the elderly in particular, policy and resultant aid have been guided by two conflicting philosophic principles (Newman, Newman, and Gewirtz 1984). The first of these principles is that the elderly are "victims of an exploitative economic and political system beyond their control" (Estes 1979:28). Therefore they should be given whatever aid is necessary to remain in their own homes. The second is that dependent elderly have "not worked hard enough" nor "saved enough" or "have lived too long," and are therefore "responsible for their own plight" (Estes 1979:28). This philosophy requires that they be "punished" by being removed from their own homes and relocated in a public institution.

In addition to the question of the removal of dependent persons from society versus attempting to care for them in a more or less natural and normal setting, another major theme recurs in the history of the care of dependents. This other theme is that of custodial care versus rehabilitation. We acknowledge that these themes are a matter of degree rather than strict dichotomies. It is also obvious that these themes or methods of care are interrelated: those calling for care in the community are more likely to be using a rehabilitation model, and to see institutions as largely custodial (as well as providing asylum and social control). Bachrach (1976), for example, reviewed literature arguing that removal from the community limits possibilities for treatment, that *avoiding* hospitalization is linked with therapeutic philosophies, and that living in the community is itself therapeutic because of social contact in familiar networks. Nevertheless, the two themes are not perfectly correlated. Some advocates have called for rehabilitation in large institutions removed from society, and other policy analysts see community care as still largely custodial. We shall separate the issues for analytic purposes, although they have been and continue to be intertwined in our social policies.

Institutional or Community Care

The "choice between care and treatment for the patient within the institution (indoor aid) and [for] the patient who remains in his own home (outdoor aid) has been the subject of frequent and sometimes vitriolic debate in almost every field of social welfare" since the eighteenth century (Pumphrey 1965:22). State mental hospitals were developed in the first part of the nineteenth century "during an era of social reform in response to the failures of 'outdoor relief' and the practice of incarcerating the insane in local almshouses and jails" (Morrissey 1982:147). By the mid-nineteenth century in the United States there was a proliferation of state hospitals for the mentally ill. In New York State, the first state asylum for the "insane" was opened in 1843. Five more state asylums for the insane were opened in New York from 1869 through the 1870s (State of New York, OMH 1986).

Nationally there have been governmental and privately supported residential services for mentally retarded persons for over a century. "Most early residential programs were large, multipurpose institutions that provided training and medical and residential care in a single setting" (Bruininks, Hill, and Thorsheim 1982:198). In 1853 the "New York State Custodial Asylum for Idiots" was opened (State of New York, OMH 1986).

At the end of the nineteenth century, although the general public did not easily accept the notion of impaired persons moving freely about in the community, better-informed persons were

aware of the possibilities for rehabilitation in noninstitutional care, and many opposed the continued existence of . . . any public institutions. In 1935, this continuing opposition to institutions influenced the framers of the Social Security Act to prohibit the payment of public assistance grants to persons in institutions, a provision afterwards relaxed to permit payments to persons in nongovernmental institutions. (Pumphrey 1965:23)

The Social Security Act of 1935 provided funds that the elderly could use to pay for boarding home care (Segal and Baumohl 1983).

Foster care for all three dependent groups has been influenced by the deinstitutionalization movement of the past thirty years, i.e., community psychiatry for the mentally ill, normalization for the mentally retarded, and the prevention or delay of nursing home placement for the frail elderly. A major reform in mental health services was the "community mental health" movement. Following World War II, the popular press (and even the movies) depicted state mental hospitals as "snake pits" that intensified mental problems rather than relieving them. By the mid-1950s "wide-spread use of . . . psychotropic drugs" expanded "the possibilities for more individualized treatment" in the community (Oriol 1980:9). In the early 1960s President Kennedy declared that segregation of the mentally retarded was "morally wrong," and "community-based facilities for the mentally retarded were . . . authorized by Congress in 1963" (State of New York, OMR undated:2). This demonstrated the "shift in the ideology of treatment for mental disability from large institutions to smaller, community-based facilities" (ibid.). Between 1967 and 1982 "the United States . . . experienced a population shift of more than fifty thousand retarded people from institutions to community programs, for a reduction in the institutional population of more than 30 percent" (Bruininks, Hill, and Thorsheim 1982:198).

Segal and Baumohl suggest several reasons behind the deinstitutionalization movement:

1) the documented negative effects of institutionalization . . . ; 2) the growing costs of institutional care; 3) [scientific] advances . . . that were thought to make the confinement and isolation functions of the institution obsolete; 4) the development of a . . . civil rights movement that emphasized . . . treatment in the least restrictive manner; and 5) the development of an extensive system of public aid that . . . created a state-subsidized market for the local provision of care by the private sector. (1983:19)

This trend away from institutionalization was supported by a political coalition of conservatives who saw community care as a way to economize, and by liberals who saw it as humane and likely to be more effective. The chief opposition came from employees of the state hospitals (Segal and Baumohl 1983).

In 1961 the U.S. Joint Commission on Mental Illness and Health issued a report advocating normal treatment in the community for the mentally ill (Oriol 1980). An example of the implementation of this policy may be given from New York State. In 1968 the stated policy of the Department of Mental Hygiene was: "Individuals would not be accepted for state hospital admission if care and treatment would more appropriately be given by another facility. . . . Patients would not be admitted when their problems are primarily social, medical, or financial or for the convenience of some other care facility" (Cumming 1968; cited in Morrissey 1982:157). Nationwide, in 1982, there were 53 percent fewer psychiatric hospital beds available than there were in 1970 (State of New York, OMH 1986). Current New York State Office of Mental Health policy is that "the vast majority of the mentally ill can be effectively treated while they continue to live in the community, if the range and mix of services available there are consistent with their needs" (ibid., p. 1).

There is much evidence indicating that the new directions promoted through the community mental health movement had inherent problems (Morrissey 1982). One serious problem with deinstitutionalization has been that many hospitalized mental patients do not have family who wish or are able to take them in (Kirk and Therrien 1975). Kramer (1970) detailed family requirements for keeping patients in their homes: patients must have a family who are willing and able to assume responsibility for their care; family assistance must be such as to contribute to recovery rather than inhibit it; and the family must not be strained beyond endurance by the patient's condition. We shall see later in this book that many patients do not have families who fit this pattern.

A problem created by deinstitutionalization has been a continuing resistance by communities to mental patients who are now in their midst. This resistance has been expressed through such community responses as petitions and zoning changes. The issue of resistance by the community to the deinstitutionalized patient is a serious one with implications for current policies and programs addressing the needs of dependent populations.

It is almost a truism that deinstitutionalization has not been accompanied by adequate substitute care in the community. Few community mental health centers have had "a well-developed spectrum of services for the care of chronic patients, such as halfway houses, group homes, foster-care programs and other residential units" (Morrissey 1982:161). Thus, Morrissey concludes:

Rather than "deinstitutionalization," a process of *transinstitutionalization* has occurred . . . over the past two decades. Thousands of former patients are now living in nursing homes, board and care homes, adult homes, and other institutional settings in the community. . . . These mostly private, profit-making concerns now serve custody, asylum, and treatment functions . . . that were once performed almost exclusively by state mental hospitals. . . . The enduring functions of state hospitals involve custody, social control, and treatment for many of the most disturbed . . . patients. (*Ibid.*, pp. 162–63)

In 1980 Oriol suggested there is reason to expect that a "swing in the policy pendulum" will recur, and "the large state hospitals will return to their prior pre-eminence" (1980:15). Recent concern over "street people" and the "homeless" may once again increase the tendency toward large-scale institutionalization.

Custodial or Rehabilitative Care

Closely related to the issue of institutional/community care is that of custodial versus rehabilitative care. Over the years the philosophy of care for those in need has gone through many changes. For the most part, in colonial and frontier America fatalistic attitudes toward misfortune resulted in providing merely the necessities for bare subsistence, rather than any attempt at rehabilitation (Pumphrey 1965). The notion of rehabilitation did not come into its own until about the eighteenth century, and even since then this emphasis has waxed and waned. We shall see in our own study of current programs that this issue is still calling for clarification.

By the middle of the eighteenth century, some of the "progressive" communities in the colonies had established almshouses. Concurrently, in the mid-eighteenth century, in addition to the helpless elderly, "children and the mentally ill were recognized as having special problems" (Pumphrey 1965:21). In 1773 the first publicly

supported mental hospital was opened in Virginia. The case for rehabilitation as opposed to custodial care was given a boost by the
establishment of the Pennsylvania Hospital in 1750. In supporting
this hospital, Benjamin Franklin argued that by receiving up-to-date
care, persons would be able to return home and resume work in
the shortest possible time, thus saving the taxpayers money as well
as benefiting themselves (Pumphrey 1965).

In the nineteenth century we find both continued use of the gen-
eralized almshouse, with a custodial philosophy, and the establishment of state mental hospitals, with a rehabilitative orientation. By
the 1820s the argument was being made that almshouses were more
efficient and less subject to favoritism than help given in one's own
home. Although the care was such as to deter people unless they
were in dire need, almshouses became the common form of assistance throughout the nation (*ibid.*). Contrary to the recommendations of "the original Poor Law that appropriate facilities be provided for the sick and other special groups, and that work be provided
for the able-bodied," the various dependent populations "of all ages,
sexes, and conditions of physical and mental health" (*ibid.*, p. 22)
were housed together in the typical almshouse or poor farm rather
than being separated on the basis of disability.

The early success of the nineteenth-century state mental hospitals
with their claims of high rates of recovery led to their proliferation.

The optimism of this era soon dissipated, however, in the throes of mas-
sive waves of immigration, the accumulation of chronic patients, and the
growing belief in the incurability of insanity. . . . Almost within a generation of their widespread introduction, therefore, state mental hospitals
were changed from small, intimate, *therapeutically* oriented "asylums" to
large, impersonal, *custodially* oriented, "warehouses"; filled primarily with
members of the lower classes who suffered from a bewildering array of
physical, mental, and social "ills." (Morrissey 1982:148; italics added)

The previous section described the impetus for the deinstitutionalization movement. In its aftermath, many acknowledged that almost no adequate treatment was being given to mental patients in
the community. Because of the thrust of the civil liberties movement, patients were "free" to be in the community—on their own,
without even adequate custodial care, much less therapeutic care.

The point was finally raised that treatment services in the community may be both less accessible and of lower quality than in the institution (Bachrach 1976).

We may briefly trace similar changes in the treatment of the aged. As Hammerman and colleagues describe, the early emphasis in homes for the aged was on custodial care. Based on "the experience, values, and social systems of immigrant groups that came to this country, [h]omes were established for those without family, the indigent, the unwanted, and the homeless to save them from the almshouse. Despite the benevolent impulse the older person was viewed as an inmate to be 'protected.' . . . He was subject to rules and regulations created for the benefit of the institution" (Hammerman, Friedsam, and Shore 1975:181–82).

With the economic problems in the 1930s, the public institution became less important, and was replaced by proprietary institutions (*ibid.*). At the same time, philanthropic institutions "became 'resources' for the aged." A more "therapeutic" orientation was developed with the addition of social services. "The 'indigency' standard gave us the inmate. The social component standard gives us the resident." The philosophy had changed from "what is good for the home" to "what is good for the resident" (*ibid.*, p. 184).

Finally, the swing between custodial and rehabilitative care can be traced for mentally retarded persons. In the nineteenth century habilation and training in state schools were emphasized in the expectation that this would enable retarded persons to return to the community as productive members of society. However, professional knowledge and skills were limited, and goals often were not achieved. The twentieth century brought a shift from "habilitation"—the developing of skills and abilities—to "humanitarian" values, the support of the dependent. Institutions that had formerly been devoted to remediation became "large custodial facilities that segregated the 'feeble-minded' from society. . . . Widespread institutionalization [of the mentally retarded] took place during the 1920s and 1930s" (State of New York, OMR undated:2).

Since that time experts have come to "agree that indiscriminate warehousing of mentally retarded people is both clinically and socially counterproductive" (*ibid.*). In the early 1960s President Kennedy declared that the "retarded must be provided with the same opportunity for full development that is the birthright of every American" (*ibid.*). Professionals now acknowledge that "many mentally retarded people . . . with the proper environmental and clinical support services . . . can achieve self sufficient, productive lives" (*ibid.*).

NEED FOR ALTERNATE CARE FOR THE ELDERLY

Despite the deinstitutionalization movement with its consequent decrease in the numbers of mentally ill and mentally retarded in institutions, there has been an overall increase in the institutionalization of the aged during the twentieth century. For example, in the mental health system Markson (1985) documents the transfer of large numbers of patients who had aged in state hospitals to nonpsychiatric institutional settings (e.g., chronic disease hospitals, nursing homes, rest homes, welfare hotels, and board and care homes). While the elderly have been deinstitutionalized out of the mental hospital, they remain to be deinstitutionalized out of the nursing home (Segal and Baumohl 1983).

Because of improvements in health care, the longevity of persons who are mentally retarded or have other developmental disabilities has increased. At the present time in this country, there are between 200,000 and 500,000 older persons with developmental disabilities (Rose, Janicki, and Ansello 1986–87). Such persons pose a particular challenge because their caretakers are frequently their aging parents, and increasingly the disabled persons are outliving their caretakers (Walz, Harper, and Wilson 1986). This population continues to grow and will need better and more integrated services (Janicki and Wisniewski 1985).

In 1975 Tobin reported projections that future cohorts of older persons would live five years longer than present cohorts and that they would stay healthier to a more advanced age. He speculated, however, that the length of their preterminal phase would be no shorter than the present cohort, thus requiring "a combination of intensive and extensive social and health services" for about 20 percent of those over age 65 (1975:32). More recently, Binstock (1985) also has questioned the hypothesis of the compression of morbidity in old age and pointed to the challenges in the 1980s in serving persons who are chronically ill or disabled on a long-term basis. Kingson, Hirshorn, and Cornman (1986) have reported that about one-fifth of the noninstitutionalized elderly have limitations in at least one major activity of daily living. The need for long-term care is substantially higher for those 85 and older.

While families are currently carrying the overwhelming share of the care of the oldest generation, structural factors in many cases prevent them from providing as much care as is needed. The prospective care giver is frequently herself in the older population and may be less able to help. Moreover, because of smaller family size in the care-giver generations, the burdens upon one or two care givers may become more than they can handle (Brody 1981). Additionally, Furukawa and Shomaker (1982) suggest that in order for older persons to be cared for by family members, as a result of the mobile nature of the population, they would be required to also move to the new location, thus sacrificing the familiar support of friends and neighbors and the well-known environment.

The large majority of the elderly do not live with children or other relatives. Lowy has discussed the rapid growth of that group of elderly who live alone "from one-sixth of all noninstitutionalized elderly in 1960 to one-fourth in 1976, and . . . from 3.8 million in the earlier year to 7.9 million in the later year" (1980:18–19). The trend toward living alone is particularly marked among elderly women and the oldest subgroups of the elderly population, the same groups who will be increasing the most in the future (Lowy 1980). It frequently has been demonstrated that institutionalization is associated with a lack of family helpers. Increased vulnerability will intensify the need for some sheltered living options.

Pfeiffer in 1973 identified three groups actively interested in providing alternatives to institutionalization for the aged: the government, the families of older persons, and service providers. According to Pfeiffer, the government looks upon alternatives to institutionalization as a way to decrease tax expenditures. The families of older persons want acceptable alternatives that will allow them escape from the guilt many experience when they see no other alternative but placing their elderly relative in a nursing home. Service providers, too, "would like to be able to match existing needs more or less exactly with available services, providing no more or no less than what is exactly needed" (1973:3).

Planners of services for the elderly for years have declared the necessity for a continuum of care and services, with a wide range of options available to fit individual needs (see, for example, Lowy 1980). For the well elderly there are the options of apartment units, retirement hotels, mobile home parks, and retirement villages (Sherman and Newman 1976; Sherman 1985). For the infirm elderly, too, there are various options: voluntary or proprietary facilities, and for those who can afford it themselves or can qualify for third-party payments, such home care options as visiting nurses and home health aides. For those who are terminally ill, choices are now available in some localities between acute care hospitals and hospice care.

Apart from those who have been classified as dependent for the greater part of their lives, most elderly persons are reluctant to acknowledge a dependency role and have expressed an aversion toward institutional care. In recognition of the need for service for persons who are between independence and the need for institutional care, several major alternatives have been used to maintain these persons in the community. One, in-home care, strives to maintain people in their own homes by bringing services to them. Another option, day care services, provides both maintenance and rehabilitative services. A third option, various forms of sheltered housing, places the client into a new setting which has needed services built into the environment.

Foster family care may be seen as one of a group of sheltered housing alternatives. A continuum of sheltered housing options, none of which is universally available, includes the following (Sherman 1985).

Retirement hotels: provide housekeeping and easy access to the services of the city, including transportation. In some, meals are provided, as well as a few organized activities such as bingo and cards.

Shared housing: refers to a "household of two or more unrelated persons residing in one dwelling unit. The members of the household share in the financial responsibilities as well as in household duties such as cooking and cleaning" (Blackie et al. 1983:1). In the "managerial model" of shared housing, the staff are responsible for shopping, cooking, cleaning, transportation, and laundry.

Congregate housing: offers individual apartments with common dining. Other support services may include activity programs, an outpatient clinic, and transportation.

Homes for the aged, domiciliary care facilities, and personal care residences: provide supportive services including meals, housekeeping, personal care, supervision, and other nonmedical services.

It will be seen that adult foster care offers some of the supports found in these other forms of sheltered housing. These include housekeeping, meals, personal care, sociability, activities, and transportation.

FOSTER FAMILY CARE FOR ADULTS

The literature is not always consistent as to the beginning dates of programs—partly because patients were sometimes placed before the program had become officially established, and other programs were official before any patients were placed (McCoin 1983). A confusion in definitions also makes it difficult to date the origins of programs.

Although historically foster care programs have ranged from primarily custodial in orientation to those that were meant to be rehabilitative (Morrissey 1967), the concept of adult foster family care we use in this book includes the provision of support services, supervision, and/or personal care. We refer to a private host family (or a single person) taking into their home a small number of adults (usually one to three, but no more than about six). Participation in the life of the family (without infantilization of the foster resident) and in the community are encouraged. Placement and ongoing supervision are provided by a public or private agency. We will use the terms "foster care" and "family care" interchangeably.

It is apparent that one problem in the development and evaluation of foster family care is that of nomenclature. Official regulations differ both from place to place and across time. Names that have been given to programs that are similar to our concept of foster family care include "alternate homes, home care, family care, alternate families, community living, community residential care, supportive living, cooperative living" (Carling 1984:5).

It is important, however, not only to indicate other names for similar programs, but to indicate the programs from which foster care differs substantially but with which it has frequently been confused in both the professional literature and the popular press. The programs diverge in size, degree of support, and outcome. Some of the residential types listed by Linn (1981) that are frequently confused in the literature with foster homes are personal care and board homes of large institutional size, community nursing homes, community residences, boarding homes, rest homes, welfare hotels, halfway houses, and community lodges. Family care should be distinguished from board and care or boarding homes, which offer primarily room and board rather than supportive services (Hill et al. 1984; Mor, Sherwood, and Gutkin 1986). In commenting on the frequent confusion between family care and board and care homes, Carling pointed out that the latter settings were "often inadequately monitored, had few systematic linkages with mental health or rehabilitation services and, in some cases, became the target for a series of scandals focused on the isolation and/or mistreatment of these ex-patients" (1984:1).

Foster care is also distinct from group homes, hostels, and halfway houses in that the former refers to care being given by a private family rather than by a professional or paraprofessional staff (Janicki and Jacobson 1984; McNeel 1965). The intent is to live as a family. Group homes also

include a service focus that has traditionally stressed habilitative activities and social therapies. . . . Foster family care placement may be used to provide for a supervised living setting for an individual needing minimal care; group home placement may reflect individual requirements for supervision as well as a range of supportive services that address their needs—either because of aging or the residuals of chronic disablement. (Janicki and Jacobson 1984:10–11)

In other words, foster care homes are more supportive than board and care homes, but frequently less therapeutic than group homes.

Another point of confusion is that a program with a single name may include both residences that are small family homes and larger quasi-institutional homes. For example, while most of the officials responding to McCoin's 1979 survey referred to those homes with one to six residents as adult foster care (similar to the homes we describe in this book), McCoin included homes that housed up to twenty residents, believing that the "augmented family model would seem the most relevant family model to apply to adult foster care" (1983:194). On the other hand, in their study of residential care homes, Mor, Sherwood, and Gutkin (1986) found that although residential care homes had as many as five hundred beds, most had fewer than six beds.

A final cause for ambiguity in literature on foster family care is that some programs are for special purpose client groups, such as the mentally ill or elderly, whereas others are for any adults (Steinhauer 1982). This means that in any one jurisdiction, the foster care model may be under the regulation of different agencies (Mor, Sherwood, and Gutkin 1986). We present the history of foster family care for three populations—mentally ill, mentally retarded, and frail elderly persons—but acknowledge that both historically and at present, the programs are frequently interwoven.

Foster Care for Mentally Ill Persons

This chapter began by tracing the origin of the placement of mentally ill "pilgrims" with families in the community of Gheel, Belgium, in the Middle Ages. Only one or two patients were placed in each foster home, and in some cases the patients were taken care of by the children of the family (Linn, Klett, and Caffey 1980). Although a mental hospital was built in Gheel in 1862, patients continue to reside with families. The hospital serves primarily to receive new patients and hold them for observation until placement; very few patients reside in the hospital during their treatment. Records of 1975 showed only 259 inpatients compared with 1,256 patients in Gheel family care (Bogen 1979).

Aptekar (1965), Bogen (1979), Intagliata, Crosby, and Neider (1981), Linn (1981), McCoin (1983), and Morrissey (1967) have all traced the subsequent history of foster family care, both in Europe and the United States. Family care programs were begun in Scotland in 1857, Germany in 1860, France in 1893, Switzerland in 1901,

Hungary in 1905, Denmark in 1909, Czechoslovakia and Sweden in 1919, and Canada in 1933 (Morrissey 1967). Other family care programs in Europe include those in Holland and Norway.

McCoin (1983) noted that throughout its long history, foster care for adults primarily has served the mentally ill, and that use by the mentally retarded and the dependent aged is more recent, although use for these latter groups has increased in the previous decade. In his review of the literature published between 1960 and 1979, McCoin (1983) cited about twenty-five studies of foster care for the mentally ill.

In America during colonial times, mentally ill paupers were boarded with private families, supported with public funds. Morrissey noted that "this was 'cold charity,' lacking humanitarian motivation. If this was the embryo of family care in this country, it is little wonder that family care, like a bastard child, has been generally ignored" (1967:13).

As we have shown in the beginning of this chapter, early American programs grew out of a dislike for the mentally ill being housed in mixed almshouses, and out of a hope for rehabilitation in non-institutional care (Pumphrey 1965). Americans such as Dorothea Dix and others, who had visited Gheel and Scotland, tried to introduce family care into the United States (McCoin 1983; Vandivort, Kurren, and Braun 1984). Another early advocate of family care in this country was Parigot (1863), who, in arguing for the Gheel system in 1863, questioned whether the best care for the insane was in large institutions (Morrissey 1967). A plan for boarding out mental hospital patients was proposed in the United States as early as 1869 in the *American Journal of Insanity* (Sherman and Newman 1976; Sherman, Newman, and Frenkel 1982).

Until late in the nineteenth century, despite the success of the family care program in Belgium, public almshouses were still considered to be the best for both the poor and the mentally ill. However, in 1885, seeking to reduce the high cost of institutional care, Massachusetts organized a program to place chronic mentally ill patients with private families, thus becoming the first state to establish a program of adult foster care for mental patients. This program was purely custodial. Over a twenty-year period, 762 patients were placed with a total of 465 families (Morrissey 1967). The program, however, slowed from 1915 to 1930; because of general prosperity families were able to take care of their own relatives, and other families did not need the extra income provided by taking in foster care clients (Bogen 1979; Morrissey 1967).

Fifty years elapsed from the time of the establishment of the Massachusetts program before other states adopted family care programs for the mentally ill. Of major importance during the 1930s was Crockett's (1934) favorable report on the use of family care as predominantly a rehabilitative resource rather than as merely custodial. The Great Depression stimulated interest in family care, both because of economic need and because this was an era of burgeoning social programs (Morrissey 1967). Maryland's, Utah's, and New York's family care programs for the mentally ill officially began in 1935 (*ibid.*), although there was a program for the "mentally defective" in New York in 1931 (Morrissey 1965). Other states continued adding family care programs: Pennsylvania in 1938, California in 1941, Illinois and Michigan in 1942, Ohio in 1945, New Jersey in 1948 (Morrissey 1967). In 1945 Pollock (1945) predicted that every state would adopt the use of family care for mental patients.

There was additional growth in the use of family care in the 1950s, and by 1963 there were over 13,000 mentally ill residents in state-operated family care programs (Morrissey 1967). Interest in family care increased further with the deinstitutionalization movement of the 1960s (Carling 1984). In 1967 twenty-five states had family care programs for the mentally ill (Morrissey 1967).

Carling (1984) noted that although in the 1970s there seemed to be a lessened interest in family care as group homes or cooperative apartment programs were developed, most recently family care homes have enjoyed a renewed interest. Some of this interest has been engendered by the recognition of the plight of the "homeless." The New York State Office of Mental Health recently has sought "to serve a broader range of residents, particularly those more severely mentally and physically disabled" (State of New York, Office of Mental Health 1983:27).

The elderly have long been found disproportionately among the mentally ill in family care (Risdorfer, Primanis, and Doretz 1971).

For example, in 1984 34 percent of the family care residents in New York state were aged 45–65, and 53 percent were 65 or older (State of New York, OMH 1985).

In addition to the various state programs, the federal government also operates a foster care program through the Veterans Administration (VA). This program has many similarities to others we are describing, but like the others it has its own history, organization, and clients. The VA has used foster care more than has any other agency in America (Linn 1981). The foster care program under the jurisdiction of the VA was begun in 1951 to serve improved psychiatric patients who needed a protected living situation (Bogen 1979; McCoin 1983; Morrissey 1967), but in 1962 the program was broadened to include medical/surgical patients "who need care and supervision of their convalescence or well-being which cannot be suitably provided in their own homes" (Veterans Administration 1975). By 1963 there were 4,000 patients in foster care (Morrissey 1967). Patients pay the sponsor directly. The program is not restricted to the elderly, and the proportion of elderly varies considerably, depending on the type of facility the patient comes from. The psychiatric patients tend to be substantially younger on average than the medical patients (Sherman and Newman 1977).

As of 1981, foster family care was used by 120 VA medical centers. Ninety-two percent of the 12,000 residents then in foster care were psychiatric patients. Between 1951 and 1981 there had been 75,000 family care placements (Linn 1981). Linn (1981) noted that deinstitutionalization in the VA did not result in an increased use of foster care (generally housing five or fewer clients); rather, the increase went to larger personal care and board homes.

The progress of family care programs, whatever their sponsorship, has been hampered by disagreement as to their goals. Morrissey (1967) argued that it was unfortunate that early advocates used cost-saving arguments for family care. Because of this stance, when family care patients were placed, chronic patients were chosen and thus a custodial emphasis predominated. Placements were primarily in rural areas, and there was little expectation of community participation. Morrissey, however, held out hope for rehabilitation and therapy. In 1965 he outlined the types of placements that could be made in family care:

1. "Intermediate placement . . . for patients who are in fairly good condition psychiatrically, but who need a base of operation to facilitate their effective readjustment to the community."
2. "Interim treatment placement . . . for patients who need continued therapy which could be conducted from a family care setting. . . . These patients . . . need a protective, supervised experience more intimately connected with the community than a hospital provides." (A large percent of this group should gradually move on either to more independence or return to their own families.)
3. "Resident placement" for chronic patients "who will probably make a marginal adjustment in family care but for whom greater freedom, individual attention, and expanded opportunity for socialization may provide a greater degree of happiness or additional gratifications" (p. 68).

Morrissey believed it was possible to progress from resident placement to interim treatment to intermediate placement and eventually to independent functioning. The next chapter describes how unlikely such a progression is for the elderly. In New York State, for example, although the Office of Mental Health family care program has temporary, transitional, and long-term placements, since family care is used primarily for the elderly, most placements are expected to be long-term rather than temporary or transitional (State of New York, OMH 1983).

Foster Care for Mentally Retarded/Developmentally Disabled Persons

Early family care programs for mentally retarded persons were instituted in New York State in 1931 (Morrissey 1966) and in Massachusetts about a decade later (Davies and Ecob 1959). Intagliata, Crosby, and Neider indicate that in the early use of family care by the mentally retarded/developmentally disabled, relatively high functioning persons were placed with rural families to help with farm chores. These placements offered benefits to both the resident and the host family. (Although not currently a primary focus, foster care still provides benefits to the host family. Today this may be regarded as an unexpected dividend.) Family care was less likely to be used for mentally retarded persons during the 1940s and 1950s because of attention diverted by the war, less need for farm workers because of increasing mechanization, and "backlash against community placement among professionals" for, among other reasons, lack of adequate supervision (Intagliata, Crosby, and Neider 1981:234).

In the 1960s, with deinstitutionalization, family care again came to be used for mentally retarded persons, and by 1966 5,700 persons were in family care in twenty-six states (Morrissey 1966). Since 1970 there has been a major shift from large facilities for mentally retarded persons (Hauber et al. 1982), and in the 1970s the use of family care increased even further. Intagliata, Crosby, and Neider (1981) cite Bruininks, Hill, and Thorsheim's (1980) estimate that in 1977 8,600 mentally retarded persons in twenty-one states resided in family care homes. In recent years family care has come to have a more habilitative orientation, either to serve as a transitional placement, or to be a less restrictive setting (Intagliata, Crosby, and Neider 1981). Like the Office of Mental Health, the Office of Mental Retardation and Developmental Disabilities also has both long-term and transitional placements. The former "represents the least restrictive and most independent living arrangement possible for a particular client." The latter is part of the process of moving clients to supportive or independent residences (State of New York, OMR 1986:10.1.1., p. 1).

The Center for Residential and Community Services, University of Minnesota, conducted mail surveys of all state-licensed, state-contracted, and state-operated facilities serving mentally retarded people in the United States as of June 30, 1982 (Hill and Lakin 1984). They found 6,587 specialized foster homes, i.e., specifically for retarded individuals, serving 17,147 mentally retarded residents (Hauber et al. 1982). This figure would not include mentally retarded people in "generic" foster care (i.e., care not specifically licensed or contracted for mentally retarded people).[1] In 1982 over

---

1. Hauber et al. reported that most of the licensed residential programs they surveyed "serve mentally retarded clients, although many other disabilities are found among clients in long-term settings" (1982:1). We will follow their convention and use the term "'mentally retarded' . . . although the term 'developmental disabilities' would be a more appropriate term for many residents." The Office of Mental Retardation and Developmental Disabilities defines developmental disability as "a

half of all privately operated residences for mentally retarded clients housed 4 or fewer residents, accounting for 15 percent of all privately housed residents (Hauber et al. 1982).

By 1984 Janicki and Jacobson were able to report that "all states operate some form of generic foster care and most operate specialized systems for certain target populations" (1984:3). In a national survey of institutional and community-based day and residential programs conducted in 1984, Krauss and Seltzer (1986) found twenty-six programs offering foster home services for *elderly* mentally retarded persons. The average age of residents was 64 years, with an average of 3.7 persons per home. They reported that the foster homes provided fewer services, primarily transportation and recreation, than any other residential type. Half the residents were involved in no day programming out of the home. The reader is referred to Heal, Sigelman, and Switzky's (1978) and Intagliata, Crosby, and Neider's (1981) reviews of studies of the effectiveness of family care for persons who are mentally retarded.

As with the mentally ill, older mentally retarded persons are disproportionately found in foster family care (Intagliata, Crosby, and Neider 1981; Willer and Intagliata 1984). Because of the history of family care as a custodial setting for mentally retarded clients for whom habilitation was not expected, and because of commonly held stereotypes that older persons were least amenable to rehabilitation (DiGiovanni 1978), family care was long considered most appropriate for the older client. However, the strengths of family care in providing integration into the life of a family and access to the community, while at the same time offering a protective environment, were also considered to be particularly beneficial to the older client.

---

disability of a person which: (1) is attributable to mental retardation, cerebral palsy, epilepsy, autism, or neurological impairment, or is attributable to any other condition of a person similar to mental retardation, cerebral palsy, epilepsy, autism, or neurological impairment because such condition results in similar impairment of general intellectual functioning and/or adaptive behavior and requires treatment and services similar to those required for such persons; (2) originates before age 18; (3) is likely to continue indefinitely; (4) results in substantial functional limitations in adaptive behavior; and (5) reflects the need for a combination and sequence of special, interdisciplinary or generic care, treatment, or other services which are of lifelong or extended duration, and are individually planned and coordinated" (State of New York, OMR 1986: 10.9.1 [rev.], p. 1).

Seltzer, Seltzer, and Sherwood (1982), in a Massachusetts study, found that of the older mentally retarded persons in their sample, 68 percent lived in foster homes and none lived independently. By contrast, of the younger mentally retarded persons in their sample, only 15 percent lived in foster homes, while 18 percent lived independently. The concentration of older adults in family care is also evident in New York State: in 1980 47 percent of the family care residents were aged 45 or above, in contrast to 30 to 35 percent of clients in other community residences. Fifteen percent of the family care residents were aged 65 and above, as contrasted to a range of 3 to 14 percent of the clients in other community residences (State of New York, Office of Mental Retardation and Developmental Disabilities 1980). Janicki and Jacobson reported that elderly developmentally disabled family care residents had more physical disabilities than their "age peers" (1984:9) in group homes, and were more likely to be without structured activities. The family care residents received fewer clinical services than those in group homes, but more than those who lived with relatives.

Foster Care for Aged Persons

Thus far we have traced the development of family care primarily for mentally ill and mentally retarded persons, and have shown that a disproportionate share of the residents have been old. The use of family care has been suggested, however, not only for elderly persons with mental retardation or mental illness but for the frail, isolated elderly as well (Sherman and Newman 1976; Steinhauer 1982).

Adult foster homes used specially for the elderly, as distinct from the mentally ill, may be traced back to the Elizabethan Poor Law enacted by the English Parliament of 1603 and brought to the colonies. Under the Poor Law, the aged and helpless poor were to be given food, shelter, and care. Arrangements were often made in colonial towns and villages for unrelated families to care for helpless individuals and to be reimbursed from public funds (Pumphrey 1965). More recently foster care homes for the elderly have their origins in boarding houses in American cities in the late nineteenth and early twentieth centuries. In these boarding houses, in addition to room and board, the guests enjoyed, for a temporary period, "some of the benefits of family life" (Bogen 1979:6). Bogen reports that boarding houses were replaced by boarding homes, with older, permanent guests. Although agencies were not involved in transactions between resident and proprietor, the boarding homes "provided the basis for a number of the early adult foster home programs" (ibid.).

According to Bogen, the first states to have programs of boarding homes for the elderly (as distinct from family care) may have been California in the 1930s and New York (especially New York City) in the 1940s (Bogen 1979). (New York City's Adult Foster Home Program initially served the elderly, and began accepting the mentally ill in the 1960s and the mentally retarded in the 1970s [Bogen 1977].) Private agencies were involved in the early development of foster care for the aged. Some of the early programs were those established in the 1940s by the Montefiore Home of Cleveland and the Jewish Community Services of Long Island. An important early pioneer in this effort was William Posner (Aptekar 1965). The Jewish Family and Community Service of Chicago began a foster home program for the elderly in 1952 (Kahana and Coe 1975). By 1964 *Aging* (U.S. Department of Health, Education, and Welfare) referred to foster home programs for older persons in Pennsylvania, Connecticut, and Rochester, New York. Since the late 1960s, foster care programs for aged clients have been sponsored by many public welfare departments (Oktay 1987). By 1975 there were forty-five states with some type of foster family care program, including fourteen states with both family care and adult foster care (Bogen 1979).

Recently, there seems to be increasing interest in developing hospital-based foster care programs for frail elderly persons who would otherwise be in long-term care facilities (SNFs [skilled nursing facilities] or ICFs [intermediate care facilities]). Braun and Rose (1986) refer to four such programs, in Boston (Dale 1980), Baltimore (Oktay and Volland 1981), Poughkeepsie, New York (Talmadge and Murphy 1983), and Honolulu. In each of these, foster families take in one or two patients. The Honolulu program (Braun and Rose 1986; Vandivort, Kurren, and Braun 1984) is under the supervision of a hospital department of social work. After six months, the forty clients in geriatric foster care in the Honolulu program showed more improvement in well-being and mobility and equal improvement in ADL (activities of daily living) skills, when compared with matched controls in nursing homes. The cost of foster family care was only 61 percent that of nursing home care (Vandivort, Kurren, and Braun 1984). In the Poughkeepsie program foster families are trained to provide medical supervision for the resident. Interestingly, three levels of patients are served, corresponding to three levels in family care for the mentally ill: long-term (more than a six-month stay), short-term (transition between hospital and home), and interim (respite between hospital admissions).

Resistance to Foster Family Care

Through the years there has been evidence of resistance to the establishment or the expansion of adult foster care. Stycos (1951) attributed the resistance to "rugged individualism." Morrissey summarized this resistance, or at least lack of interest, as falling into three categories: "1) [social and] economic factors, such as shortage of housing, periods of prosperity, increased cost of living, low board rates, a shortage of caretakers, rugged individualism and the public's anxiety with regard to the mentally ill patient; 2) lack of leadership and legislative financial support . . . and resistance or apathy on the part of psychiatric administrators and other professionals [e.g., social work]; and 3) problems related to the status of family-care knowledge," e.g., selection criteria for patients and families (1967:19). Since states differ widely in their use of family care, Morrissey suggests that the second category is most important. Handy (1968) also presented several reasons for the slow growth of foster care, including the difficulties of providing enough rewards for the sponsor, difficulties in matching the client's needs with the foster home, and interfering relatives who feel guilty that they are unable to care for their family member while others are able to.

More recently, Vandivort, Kurren, and Braun (1984) suggested that resistance to family care may stem from the family's guilt; it is easier for such families to place the relative in a traditional institution rather than admit to some other family's capability. Additionally, McCoin (1983), claiming that the family itself—both extended and nuclear—is in jeopardy, suggested that we cannot expect a strong foster family care program if the family itself is not valued.

Steinhauer (1982) pointed out several reasons for the invisibility of geriatric foster care: the variety of labels coupled with the absence of standard operational criteria; the diffusion of services (i.e., enforcement of codes, placement, and supervision); the lack of government funding which would require accountability. More optimistically, she suggested that foster care was losing its "welfare" image as the need for residental alternatives for the elderly was felt among all income groups. As another reflection of increased interest, in 1987 the first volume of a journal devoted primarily to literature in this area was published: *The Adult Foster Care Journal.*

In this book we describe 352 homes, housing approximately 1,150 residents. The residents include the frail elderly, the older mentally ill client, and the older mentally retarded client. Program managers see the greatest advantages of family care as being with a family, as well as a reversal of the effects of institutionalization and participation in community life. We will explore the extent to which these goals are fulfilled. Before turning to the field research, we present the constructs used as guidelines in our study of foster family care.

FOSTER FAMILY CARE CONCEPTS AND RELATION TO THEORY

The approach used in this book to examine foster family care is a social psychological one, that is, a person-in-environment perspective, and we rely heavily on the theoretical constructions of Lawton and Bronfenbrenner. An emphasis on the dynamic interaction between the older person and the environment acknowledges that the person is both affected by the environment and that the person affects the environment. The person-environment interaction has special meaning in the later years: one characteristic of aging can be a decreased ability to have an effect *upon* the environment, as a result, for example, of declining health. Normal age-related sensory losses have implications for safety, comfort, and social isolation in the environment.

The major concepts guiding our research were those of family integration and community integration. Because these are goals of the departments involved in placing adults in foster family care and, in a larger sense, of the theories of deinstitutionalization or normalization reviewed earlier in the chapter, these were central to our research. Our interest was in operationalizing the stated social policy into concepts that could be measured, in order to establish how well the programs were meeting their goals. We begin by introducing the actors in the adult foster care setting, that is, the persons who participated in the program. These include the agency personnel, the host family, and the residents. Next we look at familism, the extent to which the residents participated in the life of the family as opposed to being a resident boarder. Finally, we examine acceptance by and participation in the community.

The Actors

Bronfenbrenner's (1979) theory of the ecology of human development was formulated to describe the development of the child. It has, however, application to the continued development of persons of any age. Several of Bronfenbrenner's major concepts of the ecosystem and his predictive hypotheses indicate directions for study useful in our research. He refers to four systems: the microsystem, mesosystem, exosystem, and macrosystem. Bronfenbrenner defined a microsystem as "a pattern of activities, roles and interpersonal relations experienced by the developing person in a given setting with particular physical and material characteristics" (1979:22). The microsystem of adult foster care includes the care provider, his or her family, and the foster residents.

Lawton and Simon's (1968; Lawton 1970) environmental docility hypothesis contends that the less competent the individual, the greater the impact of *environmental* factors on that individual. It is the vulnerable person who is most likely to be affected by even a small change in environment, either positively or negatively (Lawton and Nahemow 1973). Because most of the residents in foster family care are frail in some respect, this suggests that the environment has a major impact. Lawton characterizes the environment as having three major components in addition to the physical: "*Personal:* the significant others constituting the major one-to-one social relationships of an individual; *Suprapersonal:* the modal characteristics of all the people in physical proximity to an individual; and

Social: the norms, values, and institutions operating in the individual's subgroup, society, or culture" (1982:40).

Applying the environmental docility theory to foster family care, we would predict that because many of the foster care residents are homebound, the elements of the home would have a critical impact on them. This highlights the central role of the family care provider, as well as the interaction among the residents. In Lawton's terms, as has been shown earlier in this chapter, the suprapersonal environment may include a mix of mental patients and frail elderly persons. Both critics of deinstitutionalization and advocates for the elderly have argued that the presence of former mental patients may have a negative effect on the life-styles of the elderly persons in residential care facilities (Sherman and Snider 1981), although the well elderly may have a beneficial effect on the mentally ill.

In Kahana's (1982) theory of person/environment congruence, a person may be characterized by the types and relative strengths of his or her needs; the environment may be characterized by the extent to which it is capable of satisfying these needs. If the needs and the environmental characteristics are dissonant, the individual can change the environmental press, leave the field, or experience stress and discomfort. Since the persons to be discussed in our book are rarely able to modify the environment or leave the field, dissonance is more likely to lead to stress and discomfort—on the part of the resident or on the part of the care provider. It may be the role of the caseworker to enhance morale by carefully matching the prospective family care resident with the home in question. The worker might also train the provider and resident to modify their needs so that they can better adapt to the environment that each creates for the other. We discuss these issues when we consider provider recruitment, client selection, preplacement visits, and matching.

Bronfenbrenner defines a mesosystem as comprising "the interrelations among two or more settings in which the developing person actively participates (such as, for a child, the relations among home, school, and neighborhood peer group; for an adult, among family, work, and social life)" (1979:25). The mesosystem could refer to the relationship between, for example, the foster family and the psychiatric center from where the resident was moved. It also could refer to the relationships between the foster care provider and the resident's own relatives. These relationships will be examined in chapter 5.

Bronfenbrenner suggests that "the developmental potential of a setting in a mesosystem is enhanced if the person's initial transition into that setting is not made alone, that is, if he enters the new setting in the company of one or more persons with whom he has participated in prior settings" (1979:211). Additionally, "development is enhanced to the extent that, prior to each entry into a new setting . . . the person and members of both settings involved are provided with information, advice, and experience relevant to the impending transition" (p. 217). This attests to the importance of the circumstances under which the transfer is made and the important role played by the caseworker.

Familism

Although the study of the family is a central focus of sociological inquiry, traditional defining qualities of families may not apply to the foster family. Furthermore, even though foster families for children have been studied, their defining characteristics may not apply to foster homes with adults, in some cases adults who are as much as a generation older than the foster provider. It is reasonable to wonder whether families that are formed so late in life might more resemble close friendships than families. It has frequently been assumed that success in foster care depends upon the selection of a provider who is a good parent (Crutcher 1944; Giovannoni and Ullmann 1961). However, good, nurturing parents might tend to infantilize older adults, contrary to accepted practice in geriatrics. To the extent that this happens in foster families, it is important to document, so that remedial steps might be taken.

A related decision requiring clarification is that between permitting the client to remain fairly passive if he or she wishes and pressuring the client to participate with foster family members in activities such as movies, church, and vacations. In addition to the close ties possible in the family setting, the advantages of stimulation and interaction to be found in foster care may be considered. Lawton and Nahemow's (1973; Lawton 1982) ecological adaptation model is useful in analyzing the fit between the resident's level of competence and the family care home's level of demand. This model proposes that overt behavior and affective response are a function of two dimensions: *environmental press,* referring to the demands of the setting, and *intrapersonal competence,* including such dimensions as health, sensory-perceptual capacity, motor skills, cognitive capacity, and ego strength. The family care provider, supervised by the caseworker, can attempt to maximize "adaptive behavior" and "positive affect" either by raising the individual's competence level or by adjusting the demands of the environment. In practice, this can mean assessing (formally or, more commonly, informally) the competence of the resident, and raising the demands to increase challenge or lowering the demands to decrase stress. Lawton and Nahemow point out that the major emphasis of most planning in gerontological settings has been to augment support rather than demand. Family care might be in a position to augment demand. Using their model, the family care home might strike the proper balance between "maximizing motivation for exercise of skills" and "overstepping the individual's limits of tolerance for stress." The necessity for supervision of the homes must be emphasized, to guard against having less stimulation in some homes than there would be in a good hospital program, or demanding more than the resident might reasonably be expected to give.

A family care home has the potential to be an accommodating environment, in Lawton's terms. Lawton and his colleagues (Lawton, Greenbaum, and Liebowitz 1980; Lawton, Moss, and Grimes 1985) described two developmental models of planned housing. In the "constant" model the setting is able to serve residents at a fixed level of capability. The residents must leave as soon as they cannot maintain themselves at that level of demand. This contrasts with the "accommodating" model, in which the housing is able to maintain a resident as his or her capability changes. The facility changes its programs, physical space, and requirements for new tenants. The Personal Care program, discussed in the next chapter, should facilitate an accommodating environment. Family care should also be able to accommodate to the client who improves while in the home.

Bronfenbrenner's theory, introduced above, predicts that "the developmental potential of settings . . . is enhanced if . . . the roles, activities, and dyads in which the developing person engages encourage the development of mutual trust . . . and an evolving balance of power in favor of the developing person" (1979:212). Trust would be implied by permitting the resident to share all space in the home with the provider's family, and adjustment should be enhanced by allowing the resident an increasing power over her own decisions. The resident has to learn to trust herself, as well.

Community Integration

The second major goal in family care is participation in community life, including using community resources and improving community attitudes. It is necessary to distinguish between simply being located in the community and actually transacting with the community. We conceptualize the goal of community integration as having two components: community acceptance and community participation. Both are necessary, and neither by itself is sufficient, for community integration.

Bronfenbrenner refers to an exosystem as "one or more settings that do not involve the developing person as an active participant, but in which events occur that affect, or are affected by, what happens in the setting containing the developing person" (1979:25). Applying this to community attitudes, or the use of generic resources, examples would be a zoning board that attempts to prevent the opening of a foster care home housing former mental patients, or, on the other hand, a local transportation authority that makes available extra bus routes to transport developmentally disabled adults from the foster home to a community concert in a local park.

Participation can mean, for example, interaction with neighbors, or more anonymous participation with the larger community. In analyzing the effect of planned retirement-housing facilities, Sherman (1979) employed the concept of site permeability. This concept can be applied to a family care home. Homes can vary from a relatively closed one (i.e., low site permeability) to one that allows for frequent penetration and movement in and out of its boundaries (i.e., high site permeability). If the home is entirely self-sufficient, low permeability may lead to feelings of security. It is more likely, however, that the resident will have to leave the home for sufficient stimulation; because of this, at least moderately high permeability is advantageous.

Bronfenbrenner hypothesized that "development is enhanced as a direct function of the number of structurally different settings in which the developing person participates in a variety of joint activities and primary dyads with others, particularly when these others are more . . . experienced" (1979:212). This suggests the advantages of encouraging the resident to socialize with neighbors and to participate in activities in the community.

Bronfenbrenner continued: "The developmental potential of a setting is increased as a function of the number of supportive links existing between that setting and other settings (such as home and family). Thus the least favorable condition for development is one in which supplementary links are either nonsupportive or completely absent—when the mesosystem is weakly linked" (1979:215). This would suggest that development would be enhanced to the extent that the care provider herself has links to the community. We shall examine the extent to which residents participate in the community independently, with other residents, or only when the provider is present.

Moving to a larger scale, Bronfenbrenner hypothesized that "the developmental potential of a setting is enhanced to the extent that there exist direct and indirect links to power settings through which participants in the original setting can influence allocation of resources and the making of decisions that are responsive to the needs of the developing person and the efforts of those who act in his behalf" (1979:256). This attests to the potential advantages of an association of Foster Care Providers, who together can influence the state agency to whom they are responsible.

After having traced the history of foster family care for adults, with its ancient origins in community mental health as well as in care for the poor elderly, we have suggested some markers in social science theory, pointing the way for our investigation. We turn now to describe the populations in our study and our research methodology.

Summary: In this chapter we have traced the historical development of foster family care for adults as evolving both from community care for the mentally ill, and from care for the poor elderly. This history was put in the context of the issues of community versus institutional care and of custodial versus rehabilitative care. While enjoying a long history, the use of foster family care has waxed and waned over the years. The need for alternative care models for the elderly was described. Among mentally ill and mentally retarded clients, older persons are already disproportionately represented in foster family care, and it was suggested that foster care might be used more extensively for the frail elderly without mental problems. Finally, the concepts that guided the research design and analysis were explained and related to social science theory.

2 · Studying the Family Care Populations

This book is based on field research with three populations of residents of adult foster care, described in the previous chapter: the mentally ill, mentally retarded, and frail elderly. The field research included three phases and took place over a period of seven years. The first study was primarily an overview of the programs, and focused on the measurement of integration into the foster family among the frail elderly and the elderly mentally ill, who were at least 60 years of age. The second study focused on the measurement of integration into the community, and included mentally ill adults of all ages (18 and above). The third study added a population of older mentally retarded persons, aged 45 and over. In order to study these three populations, we worked with three state agencies: the Department of Social Services (DSS), the Department of Mental Hygiene/Office of Mental Health (labeled DMH in the first study and OMH in the second study),[1] and the Office of Mental Retar-

1. Between the time of our first and second studies, the Department of Mental Hygiene was reorganized into two separate entities, the Office of Mental Health (investigated in our second study) and the Office of Mental Retardation and Developmental Disabilities (investigated in our third study). It is important to note that in the first study, therefore, some of the DMH homes included clients with mental retardation. At the present time, OMH and OMR homes also are permitted

dation and Developmental Disabilities (OMR). In each study, preliminary interviews were conducted with managers of the programs to determine policies and regulations, as well as to obtain guidance in drawing the samples. Interviews were also conducted with program managers throughout the research as programs continued to evolve.

STATE AGENCIES

Department of Social Services (DSS)

The first study was of two programs of adult foster family care, one sponsored by the Department of Social Services and the other sponsored by the Department of Mental Hygiene (DMH). At the time of that study the program of the Department of Social Services was a shared responsibility among the DSS, the Board of Social Welfare, and the local social services district. The Board of Social Welfare had the responsibility of "standard setting and approval and supervision of any home for adults with a capacity of not less than two or more than four guests" (State of New York, Department of Social Services 1973:2). The local county social services department approved and supervised homes with one guest. It was the responsibility of the DSS to develop "criteria for proper utilization of foster family care for adults" and to assure "that adequate monitoring of services is maintained." The recruitment of care providers and residents as well as the operation of the program, including placement, supervision, and evaluation of all family-type homes for adults, was the responsibility of the local county department of social services. Under the Foster Family Care for Adults Program, the local social services district was also responsible for needs assessment, and for help with moving, encouraging participation in social and recreational activities, and arranging transportation and other supportive services.

Since the time of our field work, the Board of Social Welfare has

---

to be certified by more than one state agency, as long as there are prior interagency agreements (Rejino 1987; State of New York, Office of Mental Retardation and Developmental Disabilities 1986: 10.3.3 [rev.]).

been discontinued. Perhaps more important, homes for one client which provide personal care and supervision must now be certified just as are those for two to four clients. The local social services district is currently responsible for inspection and supervision (both delegated by the DSS); as well as the recruitment of providers, placement of eligible individuals, and provision of supportive services (State of New York, DSS August 16, 1985).

The DSS program was designed both to facilitate deinstitutionalization and to prevent institutionalization for as long as possible. Further, adult foster care was recognized to be a temporary as well as a long-term measure for frail adults, including the physically frail, mentally confused, or moderately or mildly retarded adult. Thus, when we conducted our first study we were to find some overlap between the types of clients served in family care through social services and through the other two agencies.

The primary objective of the Foster Family Care for Adults Program was "to provide the best opportunity for enjoyment of normal family and community life" (State of New York, DSS 1973:2). Among the goals listed for Foster Family Care for Adults were the following:

—to provide services to enable an individual in an institution to return to his own home and community, if appropriate;
—to help the individual remain at or move to the level of care, between self-care and institutional care, where he can best maintain his independence;
—to provide homes within a family for infirm, disabled or elderly adults who do not require institutionalization or skilled nursing care, or continuous medical care, but do need some degree of personalized attention for their daily needs as a substitute home for the homes they have lost, can no longer keep up, or never had;
—to keep such individuals in the community for as long as possible, participating and interacting in family and community life;
—to enable such individual to function effectively in charge of his own life, for as long as possible;
—to keep such individual from institutionalization for as long as possible. (*Ibid.*, p. 9)

Currently, on a temporary basis, "family-type homes may provide room and board, respite care or care for Protective Services for Adults placements . . . if the use is compatible with the family-type home program" (State of New York, DSS August 16, 1985).

The applicant for or recipient of public assistance for whom foster care services may best meet his special needs may be [among others]:

—with relatives where relationships have become so untenable the client is threatened with being forced to leave or institutionalized, or

—on a waiting list for a private home where he wants to go and a temporary placement would prevent a further breakdown of his personality prior to finding a permanent way of living for his later years, or

—in his present home in an acute situation which demands a temporary change of residence until the acute situation improves (sickness of an adult who has been caring for the client). (State of New York, Department of Social Services 1973:10)

In January 1987 there were 872 homes licensed for one to four residents. The total occupancy was 1,478. Breakdowns by age were unavailable, but the majority of the beds were occupied by persons 65 years of age or older (Rabbitt 1987).

Department of Mental Hygiene (DMH, OMH)

The Family Care Program is described by the Office of Mental Health as providing "a 24-hour supervised residential setting and case management services to maximize linkages with community support services to persons who no longer require inpaitent care, who cannot as yet function adequately in their own homes or in other independent living arrangements, and who have demonstrated a functional level appropriate for living in a natural family environment" (State of New York, OMH 1983:28). These are "individual family homes certified to provide residential care for 1–6 mentally disabled adults" (State of New York, OMH 1986:61). The program is a major form of residential treatment and is integrated into the continuum of community living programs.

As previously explained, the New York State programs for the mentally ill were reorganized between the time of our first and second study. Therefore, for precision, we shall use DMH to refer to results from our first study and OMH to refer to results from our second study. When results are the same in the two studies, we shall refer to them simply as MH.

Similar to the DSS program, family care was recognized as both a temporary and a more permanent measure. At the time we began our studies, the family care program in the Department of Mental Hygiene/Office of Mental Health had a multipurpose design:

For some, family care becomes a temporary setting while acquiring the educational, vocational, and/or emotional stability needed for a more independent living situation. The family care experience serves as an intermediate step in an individualized program which focuses on socialization, the attainment of employment, and greater personal independence.

For others, a satisfactory adjustment in a supervised community environment will be the ultimate goal achieved. A number of individuals may require the development of skills in self-care and the activities of daily living. This will assist them in learning to do things for themselves and others and in gaining satisfaction through their accomplishments. (State of New York, DMH 1976:5).

Because the majority of family care residents are geriatric, the majority of placements are long term. Currently, the department judges that "the program is best suited to individuals in need of consistent individual supervision or long-term care" (State of New York, OMH 1986:61).

The Personal Care Program was designed to serve those residents in family care who have more physical disabilities. Providers receive more extensive training and a higher payment level. "The Personal Care Program is designed to maintain an aging family care population in their respective family care homes and to place chronically disabled inpatients who, without the availability of personal care services, would remain in an unnecessarily costly and restrictive setting" (State of New York, OMH 1983:29). Personal care services include rehabilitation services, physical and occupational therapy, and the improvement of personal care functions and activities of daily living. "Personal care patients require a substantial portion of their personal and physical care to be provided by another person but have medical needs that are not severe enough to warrant admission to a health related facility" (Carling 1984:54).

On December 1, 1986, the number of family care clients was 2,103 (Rejino 1987). In 1984 34 percent of the family care residents were aged 45–64 and 53 percent were 65 or older (State of New York, OMH 1985).

Office of Mental Retardation and Developmental Disabilities (OMR)

The Office of Mental Retardation and Developmental Disabilities relies heavily on the process of normalization—the return of skills usually lost to long-term patients. The family care program provides "care for clients who do not require residential care and treatment in a developmental center or other restrictive residential placement but who are unable to function adequately in their own homes or in independent living arrangements in the community" (State of New York, OMR 1986:10.1 [rev.], p. 2). Family care is seen not only as a place to live, "but also as contributing to part of the total treatment and rehabilitation process" (*ibid.*, 10.1.1, p. 1).

Regarding specifically their older developmentally disabled clients, the OMR states that "the elderly developmentally disabled person should have the same options available for accessing services as the non-developmentally disabled person in pursuit of personal growth and development throughout life." They further propound the "desirability of accessing generic community resources to the fullest extent possible" and the "responsibility of care providers to present a favorable image of the elderly developmentally disabled individual in the community setting" (State of New York, OMR 1983:39).

As of January 30, 1987, there were 3,337 clients in family care homes; 32 percent of these clients were aged 45–64, and 19 percent were 65 or older (Tesiny 1987). The OMR also has an active Personal Care Program.

DATA COLLECTION

Obtaining Samples

In the first study (DSS and DMH) homes were drawn from twenty-three counties in northeastern New York, the area of the state then designated as the catchment area of the Gerontology Institute at the State University of New York at Albany. Lists of homes were provided by the regional office of the Board of Social Welfare and by the family care coordinators of six psychiatric centers. In the second study (OMH) homes were from the catchment areas of two psychiatric centers, one a rural area in northern New York and the other an urban area in central New York. These were selected for contrast because of our particular interest in community integration. Lists of homes and clients were provided by the family care co-ordinators of the two psychiatric centers. In the third study (OMR), in order to be able to generalize to the state as a whole, homes were drawn from across the entire state. Lists of clients were provided by the staff of the New York State OMR and by the regional family care coordinators.

The contrasting areas of study 2 (OMH) are typical of the contrast in types of places in New York State in which family care residents are found. The catchment area of the rural facility is comprised of five counties. Much of the area is part of a forest preserve and is sparsely populated. The city in which the rural psychiatric center is located and where most of the clients in the study live had a population of 14,554 at the time of our study. In contrast, the city in which the urban psychiatric center is located had a population of 91,611, and the metropolitan area that surrounded it had a population of 340,670. The two groups of homes were found to differ significantly with regard to the accessibility of resources and services and their use by the residents. Both access and use were higher in the urban homes.

Interviews and Records

Interview schedules were constructed for each study, in each case building upon the previous study and upon input from the program staff. In the first study, face-to-face interviews were conducted with the care providers. In the second study, in order to obtain a more comprehensive picture, interviews were conducted with both the provider and the resident. Resident data on the number of previous inpatient days, diagnosis, and level of education were obtained from the psychiatric center. Finally, because of the greater distances in a statewide sample, in the third study telephone interviews were conducted with the providers. Additional data (resident functional abilities, language, disabilities, and program attended) were obtained from the central office.

Interviewer training for all three studies included role play and supervised interviews. The provider interview schedule used in the second study may be found in the Appendix. Interview schedules used in the first and third studies, as well as the interview schedule used for the residents in the second study, were similar though not identical to that shown in the Appendix. (For example, the first and third interviews had more items on family interaction; the first interview also included more items on agency interaction. Nevertheless, the second interview is largely representative of all three surveys.) Interview topics included demographics for clients and providers, characteristics of the community, measures of familism, measures of community integration, and relationships with sponsoring agencies.

Because of the differences just described in samples, methodologies, and interview items, we have exercised caution in interpreting differences among the programs. We turn now to the characteristics of the homes, care providers, and residents.

CHARACTERISTICS OF THE HOMES

Great similarity in the homes was found across the three populations (DSS, DMH/OMH, and OMR). The average number of residents per home was between 2.9 and 3.4 across the three studies, with about 15 percent of the homes having only a single client.[2]

Because we were interested in the effect of age homogeneity in the suprapersonal environment, we examined the age spread within the homes in our samples. In the first study we defined age-segregated homes as those with all residents aged 60 or older, and found that this accounted for 60 percent of the DSS homes and

2. Since the Board of Social Welfare limited the number of persons placed in family-type homes to four, in the first study we included in our DMH sample only homes with no more than four clients. In the other two studies, about 20 percent of the homes had more than four clients (similar to the homes studied by Intagliata, Willer, and Wicks [1981]). Since 1976 no new homes in OMH are certified for more than six clients. Currently no new OMR homes are certified for more than four clients, and as vacancies in the larger homes occur, the certified capacity is reduced (State of New York, Office of Mental Retardation and Developmental Disabilities 1986).

one-quarter of the DMH homes. The remainder of the homes, termed age integrated, included residents both older and younger than 60. Because the providers in study 1 noted the same differences in their residents as there are among the general population, i.e., considerable differences in the needs and interests of, for example, a 65-year-old and an 80-year-old, in the second and third studies we defined age-segregated homes as having less than a 15-year spread between the ages of the oldest and youngest residents. Any homes with residents at least 15 years apart were considered age-integrated. Again, about one-quarter of the homes were age-segregated. A later chapter will examine the effect of age homogeneity upon community integration. Segregation by sex was more pronounced, with most of the homes housing either all women or all men.

It is important to know the location of the homes in order to learn whether integration into the community is feasible. Most of the homes were in residential areas. The three populations were similar in that over 50 percent of the homes were located in rural areas (with 68 percent in the DSS homes). The DMH homes used in the first phase of our study were most likely to be in urban areas (52 percent), while the OMR homes (most representative of the state) tended to have the highest proportion of homes in suburban areas (34 percent). This locational difference will need to be kept in mind when considering community integration.

Not surprisingly, given the rural and suburban natures of the samples, no more than half the homes reported a system of public transportation in their communities, and even then, this transportation did not provide service to all community facilities. However, approximately half the homes were an easy walk to a restaurant, bar, place of worship, and barber or beauty shop. Problems with accessibility will be considered when we discuss integration into the community in chapter 4.

CHARACTERISTICS OF THE PROVIDERS

When we consider characteristics of the providers, we again find remarkable similarity across the three populations. The average age of the providers ranges from 54 to 57 across the studies, but there is a wide age range in all three service systems, with providers ranging from age 27 to 82. This alone would imply different role relationships with the clients.

The overwhelming majority (about 95 percent) of the respondents to our interviews were female. About 60 percent of the providers were married, with another quarter widowed. As shown in table 2.1, the households headed by a married couple tended to be evenly split between those with and without children. Results in the first study are presented separately for the DSS-sponsored and for the DMH-sponsored homes. (This separation will be followed in subsequent tables.) Although departmental regulations call for placement in a "family," fewer than 30 percent of the 352 homes provided placement in families consisting of a husband, wife, and child. The percent with this structure was highest in the DSS homes and lowest in the DMH homes. If we include married couples without children as providing at least the rudiments of a family, then another quarter of the homes may be included. If, in addition, we add another 11 percent of the homes in which the caretaker's child was present, though no spouse was included, we have still not accounted for about one-third of the homes.

When we speak about familism and providing a foster family, it is noteworthy that in about one-fifth of the homes, the provider had no other family members in the home; i.e., it was the addition of the foster care client(s) that created a family. Oktay and Volland (1981) reported that one of the motivations to become a family care provider in their program was a sense of loneliness. In our studies we found somewhat of a tendency on the part of providers who had

Table 2.1
Household Composition of Family Care Providers (%)

	Study 1		Study 2	Study 3
	DSS	DMH	OMH	OMR
Married couple and child(ren)	37	23	28	26
Married couple only	16	29	27	28
Provider and child(ren)	10	21	9	11
Provider only	19	15	27	19
Other	18	12	9	16

no other relatives in the household to have only a single client, affording, perhaps, something of a symbiotic relationship.[3] About a quarter of the providers who lived alone had only one client, whereas only about one-tenth of those with other family members had only a single client.

About half the providers were high school graduates, and another fifth reported having had at least some college. According to program managers, many of the providers had relevant backgrounds, either professional (LPNs, aides in hospitals, nursing homes, community residences, developmental centers) or nonprofessional (had family members with mental illness or mental retardation). Care providers were long-term residents of their communities, with three-quarters having lived in the community at least ten years. Indeed, half had lived in the community over twenty years. Their average length of time with the program ranged from three months to forty-five years, with the median being about six years.

These provider characteristics are similar to the profile reported by Intagliata, Willer, and Wicks (1981) in their study of family care homes for the mentally retarded in New York state. All seventy-seven of the providers in their sample were female, and their average age was 55; 69 percent were married; 43 percent had less than a high school diploma; and 14 percent were college graduates.

CHARACTERISTICS OF THE RESIDENTS

Table 2.2 compares the resident characteristics in the three studies. The age distributions, of course, are different because of the different designs of the three studies. That is, the first study was restricted to persons aged 60 and over. The second study sampled adults from 18 upward. The third sampled adults 45 and over. Nevertheless, even in the first study, the median age of the DMH clients was 67, while it was 82 for the DSS clients. (In fact, in the fifty DMH homes, housing 97 clients over 60, there were an additional 47 clients under age 60. In the DSS homes, with 135 clients over 60, there were only 18 clients under 60.)

---

3. It is likely that single providers have smaller dwellings, and it is also possible that housing multiple clients requires some help from other family members.

In the DSS, DMH, and OMH homes, nearly three-quarters were female, whereas only 58 percent were female in the OMR homes. According to program managers, the agencies do not have a policy about segregation by age, sex, or diagnosis. They attempt to fill the wishes of the providers. The only exception would be the Personal Care homes where providers are paid more to serve persons who are more disabled.

The modal marital status of the residents was widow in the DSS

Table 2.2
Characteristics of Residents

	Study 1		Study 2	Study 3
Age	DSS	DMH	OMH	OMR
(Median)	(82)	(67)	(63)	(62)
18–29	—	—	5	—
30–44	—	—	18	—
45–59	—	—	19	43
60–65	13	45	14	19
66–70	12	19	17	12
71–75	6	14	9	12
76–80	15	9	11	9
81–85	19	11	5	4
86–90	19	2	2	0
Over 90	16	0	0	1
Marital status				
Married	5%	2%	6%	not
Widowed	69	37	16	asked
Divorced/separated	4	9	21	
Never married	22	52	57	
Education				
6th grade or less	15%	17%	23%	not
7th–9th grade	19	28	28	asked
10th–12th grade	42	35	36	
College (some or all)	21	15	8	
Other	3	5	5	
Time in home				
Less than 1 year	31%	23%	18%	10%
1–2 years	27	10	21	15
2–5 years	30	45	24	27
More than 5 years	12	22	37	48

system, whereas in the MH system over half had never been married. This is congruent with Kramer, Taube and Redick's (1973) finding that most admissions to mental hospitals are from the never married, separated, divorced, or widowed. Although two-thirds of the OMH residents and 38 percent of the OMR residents had a relative living within a two-hour drive of the family care home, contact with relatives was rare for about 80 percent of our sample. Recent interviews with program managers corroborate the limitations of the "natural" family for all three populations. This will be discussed further in chapter 5. (The only exception are those DSS residents who are in the homes only temporarily and return to relatives' homes. Overall, this was not common.) The foster family offers the only effective family for most family care residents. This highlights the importance of enhancing familism in the foster home.

Modal education among DSS and OMH residents was tenth through twelfth grade. When information was available, and when residents had held jobs, it appeared that most residents had been in unskilled or semiskilled occupations.

Prior to placement in these foster homes, about 10 percent of the OMH and OMR residents had lived in the neighborhood. Recent interviews with program managers of the three programs indicate that despite the difference in agency auspices, most of the elderly residents have come from institutions. We found, for example, that residents in our second study had been institutionalized an average of five years in the period since 1965.

An important contrast was found between the DSS and DMH populations in our first study. Just prior to coming to the family care homes, 40 percent of the DSS residents had lived in their own homes and another 25 percent had lived with relatives or friends. In comparison, three-quarters of the DMH clients had come from an institution. The groups, however, were not completely distinct, as 20 percent of the DSS residents had come from institutions, and 22 percent of the DMH residents had come from DSS homes. This is an illustration of the practice at that time of placing deinstitutionalized DMH clients in DSS homes, including the large "adult homes" not studied in this research. It is also possible that some DMH clients were deinstitutionalized from state facilities, became clients of DSS, and were then placed in DSS homes. In other words, some DSS residents may have come indirectly from DMH institutions.

For example, the home of Mrs. L. (a 60-year-old woman living with her spouse and children) was licensed by DSS, but all the residents were from the state psychiatric center. They included two men aged 76 and 69, one woman aged 62, and one resident younger than 60. According to Mrs. L., she "advertised for boarders and the hospital contacted me." Mrs. N., a 76-year-old widow, had three women living with her, aged 80, 66, and 63. Her home was licensed by DSS. The oldest resident came from another DSS family care home, but the other two came from the state hospital. Of the six previous residents who had left her home, five went to the state hospital and one went to another DSS family care home. At least in this geographic area, there seemed to be a great deal of exchange between the two systems at the time of our first study, although at present the systems are more distinct (Rabbitt 1987).

Across the three studies, the median length of stay in the family care home was between two and five years, although many residents had lived in the home for more than five years (the range was from three weeks to over twenty years).[4] If family care residents are classified according to where they have spent most of their adult lives, we find three major groups. The first group includes persons placed in family care many years ago, when they were considerably younger. This group is likely to be thought of by the provider and her family as family members, who can remain with the family until some sort of institutional care is necessitated or until death.

The second group includes those who have been institutionalized for many years, who have indeed aged in the institution. Special effort will have to be expended if these persons are to be a part

4. The differences between the first study and the other two may be an artifact of the sampling procedures. In the first study *homes* were sampled, making it possible to study residents who had been there a very short time. In the second and third studies, which began with lists of *residents* in homes, because of a lag between listings and our sampling procedures, residents who had arrived in the period after we received the list but before we arrived in the field were not in the sample.

of the family. Perhaps both the host family and the client will need training, under the supervision of the caseworker. The clients would likely have the characteristics noted in those long institutionalized, and would need more assistance in adjusting to "the community."

The third group includes those who have been living independently in the community until fairly recently. A subgroup of these may have been hospitalized only long enough to have their medications stabilized before being placed in family care. This last group might be under some stress from having had to make two transitions in a short time, but presumably would not have lost their "community" skills. It might be desirable if the short-term hospitalization could be avoided, thus perhaps enabling the resident to avoid the stigma of being labeled a "mental patient."

Each of the above groups would have different needs in the family care home, particularly as foster family care for the elderly is not usually a way station toward independence. For older clients family care appears to be more commonly used as a postinstitutional placement, and secondarily to delay institutionalization. According to program managers, many residents finally leave foster family care to go to skilled nursing facilities or health-related facilities, or to return to institutions (psychiatric or developmental centers). Many others will remain in foster care until their death, since family care, in Lawton's terms, has the potential to be an accommodating environment, i.e., to modify its demands as the person's capability changes.

Different measures of abilities were used in our studies to fit the different types of clients. We did not have a measure of functional ability in our first study. However, in the second study (OMH) a scale measured how the resident performed, independently or with reminders, fourteen tasks of daily living. Table 2.3 presents the skills used by the residents at the time of our study. The picture that emerges describes residents of the family care homes as generally able, with some reminders, to perform most of the basic functional tasks of daily living. In the opinion of the care providers, many residents could perform most of these tasks independently at admission. In all functional areas addressed, mental health clients were seen as having increased in ability during their stay in the family care home, yet still capable of improvement. The skill areas where

Table 2.3
Activities of Daily Living Skills (%) (at present)

	Study 2		Study 3	
	OMH[a]		OMR[b]	
	Independently	With reminders	Independently	With assist or training
Follows a schedule	84	11		
Takes care of appearance	59	36		
Has sense of responsibility toward possessions	76	18		
Uses socially acceptable manners	70	24		
Knows day and month	84	7		
Has sense of responsibility toward others	72	14		
Makes decisions	63	19		
Gets around neighborhood without confusion	81	0		
Carries on a conversation	71	10		
Does shopping (uses stores)	68	13	18	43
Knows basic current events	70	6		
Initiates conversations	70	3		
Handles own spending money	55	16		
Uses saving account			4	22
Uses checking account			1	9
Uses telephone	56	5	16	38
Manages eating			90	9
Manages toileting			87	12
Manages dressing			70	29
Uses laundry			9	32
Uses stove			5	32

[a]N ranged from 95 to 101, because of missing data. Sum score comprised of all 14 items, with independent performance of tasks scored as positive response and inability or performance with reminders constituting negative response, could range from 0 to 100. Mean = 70.2.

[b]N ranged from 134 to 143, because of missing data. Sum score comprised of phone, stove, shopping, and laundry could range from 0 to 100, with independence or assistance/training scored as positive response and inability scored as negative response. Mean = 48.46.

incoming residents seemed weakest include having a sense of responsibility toward others; making decisions; carrying on conversations; shopping; knowing basic current events; initiating conversations; handling their own money; and using the telephone. In the view of the care providers, the current functioning ability remains lowest in the last two areas.

It was found in the second study that resident functional ability both in the present and at the time of admission to family care was positively correlated with the accessibility of the family care home. Further, it was found that the levels of resident ability differed among the two study sites, with the mean ability score being significantly lower for residents in the rural catchment area. The importance of choosing among rural, urban, or suburban living in order to maximize person-environment congruence was noted even four decades ago: "For some patients, especially those for whom no further improvement can be expected, the rural home is appropriate in that it is quiet and not too exciting. For the convalescent patient, on the other hand, the urban or suburban community is preferable as offering better opportunity for occupation and socialization" (Maletz 1942:600). More recently, Segal and Aviram (1978) asserted that the most impaired clients are placed in rural settings for custodial care, whereas those clients with a greater potential for rehabilitation are kept in homes near the psychiatric center (usually in a more urban setting). Our findings substantiate this. To the extent that this selective placement is true, such a policy has serious ramifications for expectations for community integration in certain communities.

With respect to behavioral ratings, only 5 percent of the residents were described by providers as often or always exhibiting strange behavior in public, or hostile behavior that could be perceived by the community as threatening. Two less socially threatening behavioral characteristics (withdrawal and confusion) were somewhat more common, but even they were exhibited "often or always" by only 13–14 percent of all residents. Despite what appears to be a reasonably high functional level and long-term residence in the community, almost no residents in the second study (OMH) were employed in the community at large, and only about one-third were employed in sheltered workshops.

Among the OMR population (the third study), 9 percent of the residents were profoundly retarded, 25 percent severely, 28 percent moderately, 29 percent mildly, and 9 percent normal or borderline. Fifteen percent had epilepsy or cerebral palsy. Ninety-five percent had no significant psychiatric disability. Concerning speech skills, 62 percent were judged to use appropriate speech, while another 31 percent had only enough speech skills to indicate their needs. Forty percent were able to understand complex statements and instructions, while another 58 percent were only able to understand simple statements.

With regard to functional abilities, as shown in table 2.3, at least three-quarters of the residents could perform self-care skills such as eating, toileting, and dressing independently. There was, however, greater variation in ability to perform the other independence skills. Slightly more than half of the residents were able to shop or use the phone, either independently or with assistance. In contrast, more than half could not do laundry or use a stove to prepare a meal, either independently or with assistance. Most residents were completely dependent on others for the use of savings and checking accounts. The inability to use the phone could have safety implications, suggesting that more attention be given to the development of this skill for both OMH and OMR residents.

It is clear that the residents of foster family care represent a great diversity in functioning (see also Willer and Intagliata's (1984) similar findings in a study of family care for mentally retarded persons in New York State). Limitations can relate to language or be of a physical nature. For example, Ms. T. (aged 64) is very limited physically. She has trouble with her legs, back, and heart. She cannot do anything without the provider's help. Ms. T. and the other resident in that home, aged 73, are Personal Care clients. On the other hand, Ms. R. (aged 70) serves as a foster grandparent, and sees her foster family twice a week.

In another family care home the interviewer noted: "This resident (aged 66) has real communication problems. Even when she's involved in an activity, it's hard to determine if she's participating or only there in body." The resident was placed in an institution at age 4. The provider commented: "Despite [communication] problems, Ms. D. uses alternate methods of communication with the family. She's babied by the other residents. Several neighbors have noticed how much she's progressed and have commented about this to me and to Ms. D." In another home, the four residents, aged 91, 82, 81, and 80, were in the TV room, but the provider said only one of them "knows what's on TV."

Finally, in another home, the provider commented that the interview did not "pick up" the extensive gains both of the residents had made since coming to live with her. (The sampled resident was a 74-year-old woman who had lived there seven years; the other was a 48-year-old woman.) Thus, we see diversity from home to home, in both the functional level of the clients placed in the homes, and in the gains and losses that the client experiences while in the foster family home.

On the one hand, one should be cautious in comparing across the three populations, since the study methods varied from study to study. Furthermore, there could be cohort differences, as the studies covered a period of seven years. For example, departmental enforcement may have become stronger (or more lax) over this period. On the other hand, given all this diversity, it is noteworthy how consistent the findings are from study to study. From the preceding descriptions it can be observed that foster family care for adults appears remarkably similar regardless of the population or the sponsoring agency.

Intagliata, Willer, and Wicks (1981) have commented that most studies of the community adjustment of formerly institutionalized mentally retarded persons tend to use a single criterion of success, namely, recidivism. Furthermore, this criterion is treated merely as a dichotomy, that is, the person either remains in the community or is reinstitutionalized. Little attention is paid to the quality of adjustment. Moos has advised: "We wish to hold sheltered care settings 'accountable,' but we have no common standards against which these settings can be evaluated. Procedures by which the characteristics of sheltered care settings can be measured may allow us to develop a broader and more relevant set of standards than those currently used for government inspection and licensing" (1977:11).

We now proceed to describe how we studied the extent to which program expectations are being met, beginning with expectations of family integration, followed by an examination of community integration.

Summary: This chapter described the field research with three populations of residents in adult foster care—the frail elderly, mentally ill, and mentally retarded—and presented the missions and goals of each agency responsible for their placement and support. The field research included three phases and took place over a period of seven years. A description of the design of the study was followed by an overview of the residents, their foster families, and their microenvironments. It was found that regardless of the program auspices, foster family care for adults looks remarkably similar with respect to home and provider characteristics. The average number of residents per home was somewhat higher than three. Over half the homes in each population were located in rural locations. The average age of the providers, nearly all of whom were women, was in the 50s. About 60 percent of the providers were currently married, and about half were high school graduates. About 70 percent of the residents were female. The residents represented a diversity in functional abilities. Family care residents may be classified into three groups according to where they have spent most of their adult lives: those who were placed in family care many years ago; those who have been institutionalized for many years; and those who had been living in the community until fairly recently.

3 · Family Life in Adult Foster Care

Although family care incorporates additional program goals such as involvement with the community and the development of personal skills, the basic requisite is that the home provide a family atmosphere. One of the primary attributes of the program is that, in addition to providing a protective environment, it simulates life within a "family." In this way, the hope is that family care homes can resocialize the individual who might be or has been depersonalized in a "total institution" (Goffman 1961). New York State's social philosophy for supervised family care homes is rehabilitative rather than merely custodial; one of the prime features of these foster family homes is participation as part of the family.

Bruininks, Hill, and Thorsheim have defined a foster home as "a family residence owned or rented by one or more persons who constitute what is commonly called a family, in which the family incorporates generally no more than six (disabled) children or adults into their family group. These (disabled) persons *live with the family as family members sharing the same home and participating in the same activities as other family members do*, within the limits of their ability" (1980: 4, italics added; quoted in Janicki 1981). Thus, two elements are present in this microsystem, an introduced resident and a host family.

As described in the previous chapter, the elderly resident in foster family care is apt to have had one of three histories, depending on chronicity, and can perhaps expect one of two futures. The resident may have been in foster care for many years. Nearly one-third of our clients had lived in their present home for over five years. Such residents may be sufficiently adjusted to this type of care. A second possibility is that a resident was institutionalized for many years (in a psychiatric hospital or developmental center) and only recently placed in foster family care. Third, a resident may have been recently placed in foster family care from the community. For Department of Social Services homes this may even include older persons relocated because of urban renewal, aged or disabled persons living in unsafe or inappropriate housing, or persons who are simply "frail and elderly" (State of New York, DSS, 1973:10). Many of the elderly residents in foster family care will remain there until their death. Others will leave family care for the hospital, nursing home, or a psychiatric or developmental center. Each of these types of clients may have differing needs, expectations, and abilities in relation to other "family members." (Other residents, usually younger, may leave for more independent housing. For example, Miss A., aged 30, has been in OMH family care a little over a year and wants to move out on her own. This was rare, however, in our samples.)

Several writers have discussed confusion in the minds of planners and the public regarding the separate needs of the frail elderly, the mentally ill, and the mentally retarded client. (See, for example, Bachrach 1981; Giovannoni and Ullmann 1961.) Whichever group the individuals come from, however, Janicki asserts that residents (as well as their care providers) should be "treated . . . with respect and positive regard" (1981:65). "The program should be devoid of rules and restrictions that are either demeaning or not age-appropriate" (ibid.). Janicki indicates that it is important to measure community living arrangements not against the restrictive criteria of an institution, but instead, against the characteristics of a normal family or cooperative living setting. Although Janicki's research concerned community residences that use a cooperative household model rather than a surrogate family model, his recommendations are equally applicable to adult foster care homes.

The second element in the adult foster care program is the foster family. As noted in the previous chapter, the care provider in our studies was often a single individual (widowed, divorced, or never married). In these instances, the creation of the "family" is dependent upon the introduction of the client(s). Regardless of whether or not there are other family members in the household, program directors stress the creation of an atmosphere in which patients are treated as family members participating in usual family activities— as distinct from boarding homes. As explained in the first chapter, Lawton's environmental docility theory (Lawton and Simon 1968; Lawton 1970) suggests that because many of the foster care residents are frail and possibly homebound, the elements of the home would have a critical impact on them. These elements include both the family care provider and the other residents.

It has frequently been assumed that success for residents in foster care depends upon placement with people who are good parents, i.e., who are creative, protective, nurturant (Crutcher 1944; Giovannoni and Ullmann 1961). Giovannoni and Ullmann assert, however, that regarding the sponsor-patient relationship as one of parent and child is actually a disservice, since "adult neuropsychiatric patients are not children" even though "their failure to maintain an adjustment in society certainly indicates they are adults with special needs" (p. 299).

On the other hand, occasionally charges have been made that foster homes provide no better an environment than the institution itself. For example, Murphy, Pennee, and Luchins (1972), in a study of larger adult foster homes (two to twenty-two patients, primarily schizophrenic, but not primarily geriatric), found

that perhaps only one boarder in four was involved in any household task other than making his bed and carrying his own dishes to the kitchen. This was despite the fact that more of them would clearly have liked to have had something to do. . . . I did not see in a single home the casual cooperation of cleaning up after a meal that one expected in many normal families. . . . A major reason for this seems to have been that the proprietors were not willing to help or correct an ex-patient if he was doing something wrong. (p. 5)

If the purpose of these homes was to provide a family setting, the result comes closer to that of a family with small children and a dominant mother than to a family of adults. (p. 6)

Intagliata, Willer, and Wicks (1981) assert that family care homes heretofore have been assumed to be a homogeneous class. Their research in New York state, however, demonstrated great variation in the environment provided by family care homes. Further support for this diversity comes from Intagliata, Crosby, and Neider's review of the literature regarding foster family care for mentally retarded people, indicating that

family care residents are well integrated into the family units within their homes. However, findings regarding the activities and responsibility of family care residents were somewhat mixed. The evidence suggests that while many residents live active, normalized lives within foster care homes, a number of others live with care providers who encourage resident passivity with their over protective style. (1981:242)

One of the program administrators interviewed in our first study (in which we studied clients of the Departments of Social Services and Mental Hygiene) raised a question regarding permission "for the client to remain fairly passive if he wishes. The intention is to encourage and stimulate the patient; however . . . in most cases, these are not the well elderly and one must set realistic goals."

The residents in study 2 (clients of the Office of Mental Health) were asked what was the most important difference between their life in the hospital and their life in family care. The modal response (41 percent) was that there was more freedom in family care. As one resident indicated, "I had a hard life at the hospital. It was regimented. You don't make your own choices at the hospital. Here I can go to my own church." Other illustrations of more freedom were "get around more," "can go downtown," "can play the piano anytime," "am free to smoke." Thirteen percent stated that their present living condition is more homelike. There was some dissent, however. Fourteen percent felt that there was not very much difference between the two settings.

Foster families are created to produce an expected outcome, and each of the family care programs in our study mandates as a goal the assimilation of the clients into the family unit and participation in normal family activities. Specific guidelines, however, are difficult to find, much less guidelines that are uniform from one program to the next. Thus, in order to describe the extent to which the residents do participate in "normal family activities," it was first necessary to develop an explicit yardstick by which any home could be measured; that is, to operationalize the fulfillment of program goals.

At the outset of our first study (DSS/DMH) we labeled integration into the family and participation in its activities familism. However, we were unable to find an existing scale to measure the concept. In other words, there was no standard measure against which the service systems and their individual settings could be held to determine the degree to which they were "familistic." To develop such a measure for foster families, we searched three major sources: the program documents, research literature pertaining to adult foster family care, and sociological literature on families.

Examples of references to the family from program documents included the following:

Social Services: A wholesome family life in which he can expect to participate within limits of his own and the family's desires. (Watching T.V., listening to the radio in his own room, or with the family members, entertaining guests, gardening, puttering in the kitchen, garden, or workshop.) (State of New York, Department of Social Services 1973:12).

Social Services: Meals not served on an isolated basis unless he desires this or temporary illness so dictates. (*Ibid.*, p. 11)

Social Services: When physically able, and if they so desire, guests may participate in housework and light occupations. Such participation must be for the benefit of the individual rather than service to the home. (State of New York, Board of Social Welfare undated:7)

Mental Hygiene [included mentally ill, mentally retarded, and developmentally disabled clients at the time the guidelines were established]: Assuring that the members of their household have an interest in and acceptance of the patients and a desire to help them achieve personal growth. (State of New York, Department of Mental Hygiene 1974:3)

At least one caution is stated, however:

He must not expect that a strange family will take him in immediately as a member of the inner circle of the family. Also it is not expected that all clients will want or be able to use this type of closeness. (State of New York, Department of Social Services 1973:12)

Most of the adult foster care literature addresses itself to client selection and the general characteristics of either the foster home or the caretaker. Some of this literature contains references to "familishness" or "familism" but no scale to measure the concept. One of the few relevant studies (Touissant and Butler 1967) alluded to private bedrooms, the quiet of family care as opposed to dormitory rooms, home-cooked food, and a greater sense of responsibility as indicators of family life.

Murphy, Pennee, and Luchins' (1972) study of larger foster care homes used the criteria of eating meals with the proprietor's family, interacting during meals, sharing of the sitting room with the family, participating in activities in the homes, helping with household tasks, encouraging initiative, minimizing regimentation, spending own money, enjoying friendships among patients, participating in social conversation, exchanging gifts at holidays, and having private possessions. Their study found minimal evidence that homes met any of their criteria. Nevertheless, the criteria provided useful suggestions for operationalizing the concept to be used in our studies of somewhat different homes and populations.

After reviewing the foster care literature, we turned to sociological literature on the family. It is acknowledged that this literature, of course, might not be directly applicable, since foster families are artifically created and lack many of the features of traditional families. To the extent, however, that criteria pertaining to traditional families are met, we can conclude that there is indeed something familial about adult foster care. While family care homes are not comprised of families in the traditional sense, they are intended to foster certain family functions.

Bengtson, Burton, and Mangen (1981), for example, in studying family support systems among elderly ethnic groups, used five dimensions of family solidarity: structure, affect, interaction, norms, and expectations. In Jansen's (1952) discussion, solidarity included eight types of interaction: agreement, cooperation, concern, enjoyment, affection, esteem, interest, and confidence. Klapp (1959–60) found a moderate correlation between family solidarity and the performance of family rituals. According to Streib (1978), a family pools resources, shares household tasks, offers companionship and mutual assistance, and incorporates diffuse expectations and affective bases for judgments.

Thus, moving from program documents and integrating what literature there was on foster families for adults with sociological literature, we identified four concepts as constituting the elements of a family: affection, social interaction, minimization of social distance, and ritual. To cover each of these four dimensions, several items were constructed on the basis of face validity to fit the adult foster care context. An attempt was made to emphasize reports of behavior rather than attitudinal response, in order to minimize a social desirability response set. These dimensions correspond rather closely to Bronfenbrenner's (1979) definition of a microsystem as a pattern of interpersonal relations, activities, and roles.

Affection: The following items were selected as indicators of affection: perception of the relationship between the care provider and residents and among residents, the formation and maintenance of close friendships between the care provider and residents and between residents, and continued contact with former residents by the care provider and current residents.

Social interaction: The items used to measure social interaction were the frequency with which residents engage in conversations, frequency with which cards or other games are played with provider and among residents, and the frequency with which the residents and caretaker participate in activities outside the home (such as summer trips, shopping, church, movies, etc.).

Social distance: Social distance was measured by the frequency with which the residents eat with the family, the extent to which residents share space with the family, whether kitchen privileges are extended to residents, and the extent to which residents participate in the performance of household chores.

Ritual: Two indicators were used to measure the performance of ritual within the foster family household: how often greeting cards or gifts are exchanged and how often residents say good night to each other. These are characteristics that may not even be noticed in a "natural" family. It is only in their absence that they become salient.

In the first study a factor analysis was performed on the items we had selected *a priori* as measures of familism, to determine whether the items did empirically cluster in the same four groups. Details of the factor analysis appear in the Appendix, but results as they pertain to our *a priori* dimensions are summarized here.

The factor analysis produced one factor that contained three of the affection items: the care provider's relationship with residents, the care provider's perception of relationships among residents, and the care provider's friendships with residents. We thus had some empirical confirmation that affection is an underlying theme in the measurement of familism.

The factor analysis provided strong confirmation for the existence of a social distance dimension. The three social distance items entered into the analysis—shared meals, shared space in the home, and kitchen privileges—all loaded on one factor.

The factor analysis included two ritual items, the exchange of gifts between the care provider and residents, and saying good night. These did not cluster together. Instead, saying good night loaded on a factor composed entirely of relationships among residents. The factor also included one affection item (friendships among residents) and one social interaction item (conversation among residents). Rather than being labeled ritual, affection, or social interaction, this third factor might more properly be labeled relationships among residents.

Additionally, in the first study, we asked the interviewers to give each home a global, subjective rating on familism. These scores will be reported in some of the case material that follows. We turn now to an examination of the extent to which the homes in the three populations under study met the criteria of familism.

AFFECTION

One of the ways to measure whether the homes are something other than an institution or a boarding home is to ask whether providers view the residents as part of the family or as boarders. Similarly, do residents view the other residents as family or as fellow boarders? Addressing first the feelings of providers toward the residents, we found that over 85 percent of the providers do view their residents as family (ranging from 78 percent in DSS homes to 93 percent in OMR homes). Our interviewers received the impression that the feelings of family reported by some providers toward their residents are maternalistic, even though in many cases the residents are old enough to be their parents. Some examples of this view are:

—"Nine out of ten are like kids, so if you raised kids, it's no problem."
—"If a resident creates a problem, I just sit and talk them out of it like a child. I try to reason with them, treat them like children."
—"If a resident creates a problem, I work with them as you would a child. I tolerate it as you would for a child."

One of the care providers, who was 47 and whose residents (all women) were aged 82, 78, 85, and 87, commented: "I'm like their mother. One resident calls me mother." This "role reversal" appeared to be easily accepted by the residents. However, it could be viewed as detrimental if it discourages independence in the residents. Murphy, Pennee, and Luchins (1972) also cited the common problem of foster parents treating their residents like incompetent children.

The care providers were outspoken regarding the affection they develop for their residents. Comments ranged from the fairly neutral, "You can't have a person around for such a long time unless you take them into the family" and "We share joys and sorrows," to the vigorously positive, "We are very much a family. Even though sometimes we can't participate with each other as much as we'd like, we still worry and fret over each other. If one goes out, when they come back it's where did you go, who did you see? We're a family. No relation, but we're a family. Whatever families get into, we get into, we even borrow money. Some read to the retarded girl [sic], some help with the dishes. The retardate [sic] does favors for the other ones." Some other providers' comments illustrative of deep affection and attachment included the following: "I missed the last old lady so when she died. I think about it and I start crying"; "Each of my residents reminds me of my old aunt or my mother"; "I love the residents, and if anything happens to them it hurts me."

In the OMR homes (our third study), a very high proportion of the providers (94 percent) also reported that residents viewed others in the home as family. In the DSS and DMH homes, however, only about three-fifths of the residents were reported to view each other as family, with about one-quarter responding "friend," and 15 percent "boarder." In the first study we found that the perception as family members was most common in DSS homes that housed only elderly clients (56 percent) and least common in DMH homes that housed only elderly clients (30 percent). Perhaps in the DSS homes, the frail elderly do constitute a surrogate family for each other, whereas in the DMH homes, the elderly would be the clients who have been institutionalized the longest and use foster care as a "mini-institution." Though the numbers involved are small, this interaction between program and age homogeneity of residents would seem to be worth exploring further if one objective is to promote integration into a family.

A range of responses described the feelings the residents had for *each other*. Two examples of responses indicating a great deal of affection among residents were "The residents were terribly upset when one resident had a stroke. The residents hover over with concern for that resident"; and "Two of the residents are like mother and daughter. When one went away with her family for a few days, the other was 'lost.'" These two responses clearly illustrate relationships in which there is a great deal of interrelatedness. On the other hand, the provider in another home explained why the relationship between two of her residents was more like that of boarders: "They both live in their own worlds. They both have lived alone for about thirty years, and aren't interested in each other."

One provider with ten residents referred to her attempts to "make them feel like brothers." This illustrates that she is aware of the goals of the program, and is attempting to engender familistic feelings. (Although regulations have now limited the size of the homes, it is noteworthy that family feelings can be created in homes this large—perhaps requiring greater effort on the part of the provider.) Another provider illustrated the complexity of describing familism;

that is, some members of the household may feel like family while others are either too new to the family or are not able to participate and be considered as family: "It pretty much feels like family, but one resident has cerebral palsy and the rest of the girls feel uncomfortable with her. The newest girl isn't integrated yet, she is still too institutionalized. The rest are a family."

It is interesting that in the first study so many more providers regarded the residents as family, as contrasted to the way in which the residents viewed each other. For example, in one DSS home the interviewer commented: "The children play with the residents all the time. It appears that although the family treats the residents well, and attempts to assimilate them into the family, the individual residents don't seem to be a cohesive group." The interviewer gave this home an intermediate familism rating.

Following Murphy, Pennee, and Luchins' (1972) observation that the foster family appears to resemble a family of small children with a dominant mother, perhaps a further parallel can be drawn. In the foster family several individuals may be introduced into the nucleus. As in natural families, however, most frequently the new individuals are introduced one at a time and an adjustment is made. Usually roles and rules are established before another newcomer is introduced. There may be competition and rivalry between the "siblings" (Oktay and Volland 1981; Redding 1963). However, as in natural families, it appears that there is less tension between the homemaker and the newly introduced resident than among the residents.

It is important to view the relationship between the provider and the resident as an interactive one: the provider is responding to the stimulus of the individual resident, with whom she is engaged in a reciprocal relationship. It is not surprising that providers respond differently to different residents; an important dimension of the relationship is the perceived reciprocity of affection.

The following is an example of a relationship in which there is a lack of reciprocity, and the resident's perception of the relationship is at odds with the provider's familial perception: "I usually view my relationship with the residents as 'family,' but one of the residents I have now treats us as 'hired help.' I treat residents like I would a relative, but I don't get so emotionally involved that I go into hysterics if something happens." The interviewer in this case commented: "The care provider spoke a lot of some former residents with whom she was quite close. Familism now is not that great, but in this case, it seems to have a lot to do with the resident, i.e., the one resident who views them as hired help."

In addition to asking directly about feelings of family, we asked about the development of close friendships in the foster family. This might represent a lower degree of familism; at least it is a component of affection. About 60 percent of the providers reported that they often or always formed close friendships with residents and residents always or often formed close friendships with each other. About 15 percent reported that such friendships are never formed.[1] Although they were in the minority, negative responses may be illustrated by the following: "There's really no friendship between the residents. If one gets hurt, the other might laugh. There is no respect for the other's possessions."

One of the providers who viewed the residents as family members, but who rarely formed close friendships with her residents, explained that "friendships" could be misinterpreted as preference and something to be avoided: "You have to be careful about this. Many have been retarded, and there are problems with partiality." Another provider explained her response in terms of resident characteristics: "Because of the type of patients they are, you really can't get too close. There is usually an element of protection associated with people from an institution."

Finally, another characteristic of family affection, one usually taken for granted in natural families, is the maintenance of contact with family members after some members have moved away. To what extent is this contact maintained with foster family members? Although movement out of family care is not frequent, this question was posed in the first study. About 40 percent of the care providers reported that they "often" maintained continued contact with former residents, whereas only about 20 percent reported that their

1. A number of instances of underestimations of familism were detected. These occurred when care providers were asked to identify how frequently they form close friendships with their residents. A few providers said that they never form such friendships as they regard the residents as family, not as friends. It is impossible to know how often care providers interpreted the question in this way.

residents often maintained contact with each other. This situation resembles natural families in which parents maintain contact with children even in the instances in which siblings do not necessarily maintain contact with each other. Also, of course, the providers have the whole pool of former residents with whom to maintain contact, whereas the residents only know those whose stay coincided with theirs.

The preponderance of the continued contact reported in both cases tended to be personal. Some of the continued contact was by telephone, letters, or greeting cards, but most was face-to-face (suggesting that residents do not move far away). About one-quarter of the providers reported no contact with residents after they left, and nearly half reported that residents had no continued contact with each other. In some cases, the provider continued to fulfill the role of surrogate family: "If they have no family, I make a point to visit them." Some contact was initiated by the former resident: "The person who left usually sent cards."

A range of attachment and continuity was reported. One type of contact was fairly superficial, but indicated that the former residents still played a role in the household: "Although the residents never have contact with the former residents, they often ask about them and reminisce about their time together." An intermediate level of contact was illustrated by this comment: "After a person has left my home, the other residents have me call, or they get together and send flowers or cards." Finally one provider illustrated the most permanent kind of continued contact: "Two former patients are buried in my family plot."

Two more detailed case examples illustrate the ambivalence found on the part of the provider: she knows that it is important for the residents to improve; indeed she finds this rewarding. On the other hand, she is likely to form significant attachments with the residents, and it is difficult to see them leave.

- Mrs. C., an OMH provider, is 68 years old and married. She likes to have residents who can improve. She likes younger residents so she can accomplish more, although some elderly residents have been "great." She is ambivalent about those who are discharged. "It is a good feeling to see them back to a normal life, and seeing them discharged is very rewarding," but she hates to see them go because she becomes attached to them. She visits or writes to them when they have been discharged. Mrs. C. has been in the program for thirteen years and has had approximately twenty residents. She got her granddaughter, Mrs. D., who lives down the road, into the program, and when the granddaughter went on vacation, Mrs. C. took in her resident. The interviewer gave this home the highest familism rating.

We also interviewed Mrs. C.'s granddaughter, Mrs. D., who is 28 years old and lives with her husband and two sons, aged 7 and 8:

• Mrs. D.'s resident, a 65-year-old widow, has been in the family care home for seventeen months, and the provider's two sons accept her as though she's always been there. The resident is being discharged as soon as an apartment becomes available, and Mrs. D. is "thrilled at her progress."

To summarize, it appeared that affection was an underlying theme of familism, and it seemed prevalent in the large majority of family care homes, for all three populations. This finding was apparent in the objective questions, in the factor analysis, in the free comment quotes, and in the interviewers' ratings. We turn now to the second dimension of familism, social interaction.

SOCIAL INTERACTION

On a typical day there is a great deal of variety across residents with respect to social interaction. Some do not seem to do much more than watch TV and nap. Others visit with relatives, go on errands, help out with household chores, and so on. As noted earlier in the chapter, Bruininks, Hill, and Thorsheim (1980) include in their definition of a foster home the criterion that the "disabled" persons participate in the same activities, within the limits of their ability, as do other family members. The New York State Office of Mental Retardation and Developmental Disabilities, for example, requires that the client be integrated "with the normal routine of family life . . . including recreation" (1986: 10.6.2 [rev.], p. 1). We included several such measures in our scale of social interaction.

Perhaps the least demanding form of social interaction is conversing with other residents. Overall, about 85 percent of the residents were reported to do so often, ranging from 75 percent in the first study (DSS/DMH) to 95 percent in the OMR study. In about 10 percent of the DSS/DMH homes conversations among residents rarely occurred. (The questionnaire wording in the OMR study included conversation with family members, perhaps partially explaining the discrepancy across studies.) In general, this pattern of participation is what would be expected from a "natural" family.

Much lower participation was reported with regard to playing cards or games with other residents or with the provider. As shown in table 3.1, about half never did this. Unfortunately, we did not ask directly regarding residents' ability to do so. One provider reported that the residents were not able to play cards or games with each other, but they did sit together and watch TV or listen to the radio. "One of the residents sings for the men, who seem to enjoy it very much. I sing with her, too. Also, my children play musical instruments for the residents. When the residents have a birthday, I give a party for them and invite their friends and relatives."

A second provider noted that the residents often sat on the porch and reminisced about the past. Also, the residents loved to watch the birds and other wildlife. The same provider mentioned, "We read the Bible for an hour every night." The importance of the church in the lives of some of the providers and residents has been

Table 3.1
Social Interaction: Participation of Residents in Playing Cards/Games (%)

	With Care Provider		With Each Other[a]	
	DSS	DMH	DSS	DMH
(N)	(49)	(50)	(42)	(43)
Often	29	18	14	18
Sometimes	12	10	10	12
Rarely	12	14	26	12
Never	47	58	50	58

Note: Neither question was asked in studies 2 or 3.
[a]Was not asked in single-client homes.

striking throughout our study. Bible reading is mentioned as an important activity by some. Meeting friends at church is a source of social interaction for many.

Another indicator of resemblance to a family is the extent to which the resident participates with the family in outside activities. In the first study (DSS/DMH) residents in 60 percent of the homes participated often with the family in outside activities. In the second and third studies we asked about specific outside activities in which the sampled resident participated with the provider. Results appear in table 3.2, and show some differences between the two study populations. In the second study (OMH), about three-fourths went to restaurants, and about one-fourth went to religious services, parties, and meeting places. Fewer than 10 percent went to clubs, movies, plays, or concerts. For the most part, then, at least as reflected by this set of items, they did not go out with the family into the community. In Bronfenbrenner's (1979) terms, the links to the exosystem do not appear to be strong in a majority of these homes. On the other hand, in the third study over 90 percent of the residents went to restaurants and meeting places, three-quarters to parties, one-half to religious services, about two-fifths to movies, plays, or concerts, and one-fifth to clubs. The OMR resi-

Table 3.2

Social Interaction: Participation of Residents with Care Provider in Outside Activities at Least Several Times a Year (%)

	OMH^a	OMR^b
Restaurants	78	91
Religious services	29	54
Parties	27	76
Meeting places	21	93
Clubs	8	19
Movies	6	36
Plays or concerts	9	38
Spend time with friends	19	79
Spend time with neighbors	33	76
Spend time with relatives	10	18

Note: Question was not asked in study 1.

[a]N ranged from 97 to 101.

[b]N ranged from 146 to 151.

dents were also more likely to spend time with friends and neighbors than were the OMH clients.

At this time it is not clear why such large discrepancies exist. Possibly it is more difficult for care providers to take clients with mental health problems to mingle in the community. However, the two populations were remarkably similar in activities without the care provider. Perhaps training is required to encourage the provider to take the resident to more community activities. The next chapter explores in detail the question of participation in community activities, both with and without the care provider.

SOCIAL DISTANCE

A third aspect of familism within the homes is a lack of maintenance of social distance. Bercovici (1981) reported that in the ten group homes for the mentally retarded in her study, interaction between the staff and the residents was characterized by the maintenance of social distance. The foster family homes in our samples appeared to maintain much less social distance. In the OMH and OMR studies about 90 percent reported that residents always or often ate at least one meal per day with the family. Two-thirds of the care providers in the first study reported that residents often ate their meals with the family (58 percent in DSS homes, and 76 percent in DMH homes). About one-quarter of the DSS providers reported that residents never ate with the family.[2] Although having meals separately is difficult to view as a "family" arrangement, and is counter to departmental policy (e.g., State of New York, OMR 1986: 10.6.2 [rev.], p. 1), we might note that it is rare in modern families for a family to dine together three times a day.

Various explanations were given by the care providers for why the residents were segregated at meal times. For example, in one family the residents ate at the same time and watched TV, but not

2. In the first study (DSS/DMH) the question was worded, "How often do the residents eat with the family?" whereas in the second (OMH) and third (OMR) studies the question was worded, "How often do the residents eat at least one meal a day with the family?" The fact that studies 2 and 3 only required one meal a day to meet the criterion could account for at least some of the discrepancy in positive responses between the first and the other two studies.

with the family. The provider commented that it was "hard to eat at the same table with senile people; they put their hands into others' food." A similar explanation was given by a second provider: "The residents eat with the family only on special occasions like birthdays and holidays, due to their physical and mental condition. I have to assist the residents with eating in their own rooms." A third provider also mentioned physical disabilities as reasons for the residents' eating alone. She was concerned with her residents' need to have privacy as a way of maintaining their dignity. "When they can have privacy, they eat with their hands." She explained that one resident eats alone because she is too shy to eat with the family. Also, she said, the residents generally don't have good teeth, and many are blind.

A different reason for separate eating, which is revealing about her real view of "family," was given by a provider who said her eight residents were "like family." She then went on to say that the residents never ate with the family because the family "needs time to be family."

An important component of continued development is the mutual trust among persons in the environmental setting. One would assume that trust is enhanced by permitting the family care resident to share the space in the home with the provider's family. Table 3.3 indicates that only about half the care providers in the first study reported that, with the exception of bedrooms, all rooms in the home were considered common space. The figure was about

Table 3.3
Social Distance: Use of Home (%)

	DSS	DMH	OMH	OMR
(N)	(50)	(50)	(101)	(147)
All rooms used by all	48	62	74	76
Sections for family only	12	4	12	5
Sections for residents only	0	4	5	3
Separate and common sections	18	12	8	13
Separate sections for family and for residents	18	16	1	1
Separate dwellings	4	2	0	2

three-quarters in the other two studies. It should be noted that 17 percent of the homes in the first study (DSS/DMH) reported no common rooms. A few of the providers even reported housing their residents in entirely separate dwellings.

A couple of the homes where residents spent much time separated from the rest of the family were Mrs. S.'s and Mrs. T.'s. Mrs. S., a 58-year-old widow, was an ordained minister in the Assembly of God church. Her residents, aged 98, two aged 88, and 84, were all widows. The upstairs part of the house, where the residents lived, had a gate. There was a deck upstairs, which the residents might use. Mrs. S. brought the residents downstairs every once in a while, for visitors or for holidays, when she invited their families for a buffet. Otherwise, they stayed up in their rooms and had their food brought up. According to Mrs. S., the residents "are embarrassed to eat at the table." This home was given a low familism rating by the interviewer.

In Mrs. T.'s home the resident, Mr. J., had his own apartment, which the interviewer felt was detrimental to fostering a family atmosphere. Nevertheless, Mrs. T. did seem to have a fair amount of interaction with Mr. J., and the interviewer gave the home a moderate familism rating. In another home with four residents, aged 80 to 91, the upstairs was strictly for the residents. All rooms had signs, saying, for example, "bath (no visitors please)"; "toilet (visitors please)."

At the other extreme, perhaps, was Mrs. G.'s home, where boundaries did not seem to be in evidence. Mrs. G. was baby-sitting for four neighborhood children as well as for her two grand children. The interviewer concluded that usually there would be just one infant throughout the day, with the other five coming in after school. Everyone, residents and children alike, called the provider Maude. One resident had a cat and a three-day-old litter of eleven kittens on the floor of her closet. In the two other resident bedrooms there were also cats. There was also at least one dog. While the interviewer was there the residents were sitting up in their rooms, but the interviewer thought that that was because she was there. On an ordinary day they would probably be watching TV or visiting with neighbors. Mrs. G. commented: "I never live alone, we are company for each other. They like their things. I know that they are not supposed to have so much in these places but what can you do? They love their animals."

The maintenance of segregated living space for "family" and residents is not only against the intent of the sponsoring departments, but is hard to reconcile with the providers' avowal that they look upon these clients as "part of the family."[3] It may be that this behavioral indicator is a more valid measure of true familial feeling than the self-report as to how they regard their clients. On the other hand, perhaps social distance in this case serves the positive function of minimizing conflict as well as preserving privacy, dignity, and autonomy for the residents (Lawton and Bader 1970). Aged persons living with adult children generally have less authority over domestic and financial functions. The older person may participate in the household chores but is seldom given the authority for decision making. Such older persons are less autonomous than others in the use of time and living space. A greater degree of social distance may therefore be beneficial in foster families for mature adults as compared with foster families for children.

In his study of families in the Netherlands, Taietz (1964) found that older persons living with adult children had separate entrances and ate alone. This need for separation may also account for the recent popularity of "Granny flats," a concept originating in Australia where multiple generations live in close proximity to each other. Granny flats are small, mobile, self-contained housing units rented from the housing authority and placed in the yard of the

---

3. Responses to the social distance items should be interpreted with caution. OMH regulations specify that residents should eat at least one meal a day with care providers, and there should be no rooms other than bedrooms for the exclusive use of family or residents. Thus, a negative answer by the care provider would admit failure to comply with regulations. This did produce a number of "false positive" responses of which interviewers became aware in study 2. Interviewers noted, for example, that they were aware of homes where rooms were set aside for the exclusive use of residents; at the same time, the care provider denied the existence of such rooms. It is impossible to verify how frequently this occurred without our knowledge, and we thus must assume that responses to the measures of familism based on meals and room use are somewhat inflated. In the first study we noted that providers of DSS homes reported somewhat less common room usage than in DMH homes; we cannot know whether more stringent regulations by DMH caused more sharing or more distortion of the truth.

child's home (Blackie, Edelstein, Matthews, and Timmons 1983), giving both the children and the parents privacy and independence but also mutual support. Those foster homes that do maintain separation may be attempting to achieve some of the same goals.

As noted earlier, Murphy, Pennee, and Luchins (1972) were critical of the proprietors they studied for not permitting the ex-patients to share in household tasks. In our studies, as shown in table 3.4, kitchen privileges, e.g., getting a snack or sandwich, were extended in about two-thirds of the homes. In the DSS sample, for example, there were care providers who did not permit residents in the kitchen at all, despite departmental regulations which included specifically "puttering in the kitchen, garden or workshop" (State of New York, DSS 1973:12). Occasionally a caretaker commented that freedom in the kitchen would be dangerous or disruptive for these elderly residents. It is true that one of the first signs that an older person may need some supervision is a noticeable inability or forgetfulness in the kitchen. For example, one of the residents was described as not having kitchen privileges because she once burned a two-pound can of coffee on the stove. Another did not have kitchen privileges because "he's too grabby; the other residents can have kitchen privileges if they ask first."

As a final indicator of the minimization of social distance, caretakers were asked the extent to which residents participate in household chores. (This criterion was also part of a selection checklist for board-and-care homes used by Betts, Moore, and Reynolds

Table 3.4
Social Distance: Kitchen Privileges (%)

	DSS	DMH	OMR
(N)	(49)	(50)	(151)
Yes	49	62	50
Limited	10	12	17
No	41	26	20
Not able	—	—	13

Note: Question was not asked in study 2. In study 1 the question was worded "Do the residents have kitchen privileges?" In study 3 the question was worded "Does [the resident] have kitchen privileges? That is, does he/she use the kitchen to get him/herself a snack or a sandwich?" and a code for "not able" was added.

[1981].) While it might be argued that participation by the resident in chores could be more for the benefit of the care provider who is getting free household help than for the minimization of social distance, it was judged that this kind of participation more nearly approximates "natural families" and that exclusion of the residents from such activity could be an indication of separation; that is, normally family members share household chores, while paying boarders do not.

Participation in chores, either assigned or through the client's initiative, was reported in nearly all the DMH and OMR homes. (Over 80 percent of the latter reported this was "often," while another 11 percent reported "sometimes.") On the other hand, in almost one-quarter of the DSS homes, residents never participated in the work of the household. When a reason was given, as with kitchen privileges, it was usually that the residents in these homes were perceived as being too old or too infirm (14 percent). In three-quarters of the DMH homes, there were regularly assigned chores, whereas in 44 percent of the DSS homes, chores were reported to be only on the residents' initiative.

Chores in which the residents most often participated included making their own beds, tidying their own rooms, helping with dishes, and gardening. In the matter of chores, it is necessary to individualize the expectations. For example, a provider reported: "One resident sweeps stairs, makes her bed, peels potatoes. The other one is 'a lady' and told me she didn't come here to work. She feels she is paying for that." Since family care is not simply a boarding house arrangement, this is an area where the agency can help to clarify expectations held by residents.

As mentioned earlier, the factor analysis conducted in the first study provided strong confirmation for the existence of a social distance dimension. We have seen that there is variance in the degree to which the homes have boundaries—boundaries for eating and boundaries for living space. There is also variance in the degree to which residents have kitchen privileges and participate in chores. Arguments have been made in favor of some social distance for the purpose of maintaining privacy and dignity. Some residents were not permitted kitchen privileges for their own protection, and some residents were not given chores if they wished to be served. On the other hand, in some homes everything was shared: meals, living space, and household responsibilities.

RITUAL

Institutions have rituals, both informal and formal, such as seating arrangements or initiations. Families also have rituals, as a representation of the macrosystem, such as celebrating the Fourth of July and Mother's Day, or more individualized, such as saying good morning and good night. Klapp (1959–60) enumerated twenty six rituals of descending importance to families, such as having Christmas dinner together, giving gifts to family members on birthdays, giving Mother's Day gifts or cards, going to church together, and taking a regular walk or stroll. From these, we selected questions that we thought most appropriately tap the performance of ritual in foster families for adults.

As with affection, more ritual was reported between the care provider and resident than among residents. In the first study (DSS/DMH) about half the care providers reported that the residents often exchanged cards or gifts with each other, while one-third reported residents never did so. Regarding the exchange of cards or gifts between providers and residents, which 80 percent reported as occurring often, providers explained that this was frequently one-sided because residents could not afford the gifts. Therefore, in the third study (OMR) the question was changed somewhat, and providers were asked about an exchange of favors between provider and resident, such as doing errands or getting something for the other when he or she was tired. Nearly two-thirds reported that this happened often. Again this may not be an accurate reflection of familism because of infirmity or handicap. There is a need to develop some realistic measures.

The other ritual, saying good night, occurred frequently. In the first study (DSS/DMH) the question focused on residents saying good night to each other. In the third study (OMR) the question asked about residents and family members saying good night to each other. In each case about 80 percent of the providers reported that this happened "often." The level of this ritual was comparable to the exchange of care provider/resident favors in the OMR homes, but higher than residents' exchange of gifts in the DSS or DMH homes.

As noted earlier, the items we have labeled ritual did not produce a separate factor. We might observe, however, that these homes did demonstrate some rituals that are found in "natural" families, such as saying good night. Also,the rituals seemed to be more firmly established between the provider and the residents than among residents.

THEMES IN FOSTER FAMILIES FOR ADULTS

The various measures of familism, designed to include the four dimensions of affection, social interaction, social distance, and ritual, seem to indicate that family integration and participation do occur in these foster family homes for adults. On most of the familism indicators, across all three studies, an affirmative response was given in at least 50 to as many as 85 percent of the homes. Although there was a great diversity across indicators, and from study to study, we might conclude that familism, as we have defined it, was present in about two-thirds of the homes. Additionally, the evidence indicated that the relationship between provider and resident was more frequently perceived as familial than that which existed among the residents themselves. The data also indicated some degree of maintenance of social distance. In most instances, however, adult foster care does appear to serve as a surrogate family rather than as a small institution. The next sections offer suggestions for strengthening the family model.

Enforcing Rules While Maintaining Informality and Flexibility

The needs to be fulfilled in family care are complex. As we will discuss in greater detail in chapter 5, the needs to be considered are those of the client, the provider, the agency as a reflection of the community, and sometimes the relatives of the client. Given all these actors in the setting, one must balance a variety of considerations. Oktay and Volland (1981) point out that community care homes or adult foster care are strong just where institutions are weakest. The staff monitoring these homes need to appreciate that it is these characteristics that give the homes their family nature. For example, meals may not always be served at the same time or according to a dietician's standards; rather, meals are served when the client is hungry, and fit the client's (or at least the provider's) tastes. Likewise, the standards of cleanliness may fit community standards rather than what is appropriate or necessary in a nursing home. Relationships are more likely to encompass diffuse responsibilities than rigid roles. Oktay and Volland caution that too rigid adherence to rules will make the homes more institutional, the very essence of what they were designed to avoid. The following case, which received a very high familism rating from the interviewer, illustrates the issues involved.

• Mrs. V. is 36, and lives with her husband and seven children. There are also a monkey and two dogs in the house. Mr. V. is a corrections officer in a prison. The four residents are aged 86, 85, 81, and 57. Originally, Mrs. V. became involved in the program through self-selection. She bought a large house and called the state hospital and the "welfare department." According to Mrs. V., when staff members from the state hospital saw her seven children, they turned her down. Next, the Department of Social Services called with two couples to place. The social worker told her about the new program; she applied and was licensed. "Residents have to like kids. They have to want to be in a family situation, not just want to sit in their room and rot. I expect them to have a 'little sass.'" At present there is one problem woman they are trying to remove. Mrs. W. (resident) has physically attacked the other residents. Last week Mrs. W. attacked Mrs. V. with a cane, and Mrs. V. slapped Mrs. W.'s "bottom." Mrs. V. was very upset; she had to hit her. Before, when Mrs. W. became vicious, Mrs. V. splashed her with cold water, which worked. Mrs. W. is under medication and a private client, therefore harder to "get rid of." Mrs. V. is "fed up now" because of the problem resident. "The joy has gone out of it" because Mrs. V. can't leave the house. Mrs. V. is sure they're going to close her down. The inspectors told her the house "had to be like a motel or restaurant as far as cleanliness. I tried to keep it spotless for a while but the residents complained they didn't see enough of me because I was always cleaning. With seven kids spotlessness is impossible." Mr. and Mrs. V. want to be more therapeutic than custodial. "The agency is more interested in rules rather than the care of residents. Residents are ignored. We could have saved the state money if they had left the cancer victim here. The rules are not at all flexible." The interviewer commented: "There is a very warm feeling in this lively home. Both Mr. and Mrs. V. seem to enjoy elderly who have 'some life in them.' It'll be a pity if they go out of the business."

Providing Challenge in the Environment of Family Care

Another issue related to strengthening the family nature of these homes involves expecting the highest possible level of functioning from the residents. In Lawton and Nahemow's model (1973) the family care home might strike the proper balance between "maximizing motivation for exercise of skills" and "overstepping the individual's limits of tolerance for stress." They point out that the major emphasis of most planning in gerontological settings has been to augment support rather than demand. In some homes, even though the residents are capable, the provider runs the bathwater for them, fixes their snacks, and so on. Family care might be in a position to augment demand, that is, to stimulate the resident to relearn or continue to use skills necessary for daily interpersonal interaction.

Expectations regarding family interaction should be communicated to the provider, and more effort could be expended on the part of the caseworker, supplemented by training where necessary, to encourage such interaction. Familism on the part of care providers frequently appears to be maternalistic—much as if they were housing foster children. training should emphasize different expectations for adults in foster care than for children. We have also suggested that providers might do more to encourage social interaction with the family outside the home.

In those instances where it is determined that a minimization of social distance would be beneficial for the resident and the care provider, providers could be encouraged to give residents more opportunity to help with at least some minor chores. Otherwise we find behaviors similar to the way children are treated, where the homemaker often finds it easier to perform certain tasks herself than to take the time to encourage the development of the necessary skills. If family affection and interaction are to occur, residents and care providers should share some common living areas in the house and certainly should not be housed in separate buildings. Eating together for at least one meal each day should be encouraged as part of "family life." Rationalizations such as "embarrassment" on the part of either the resident or the host family should not be necessary.

For some residents, a personalized link may be necessary to facilitate integration into the community. Perhaps foster family care can help to allay some of the anomie experienced by the discharged long-term mental patient who, when deinstitutionalized, has to replace norms with which he has lived for years. As one provider said: "The first two years in the program it's very difficult. They don't know how to live in a family situation, and it takes them a long time to adjust." Since the family care provider is herself integrated into the neighborhood, as contrasted to professional caretakers in other community placements, the foster family can serve more naturally as a liaison between the elderly resident and the community. For other dependent elderly residents, perhaps we should not think of the family as the *link* to the community as much as *constituting* their community. We turn to a further consideration of this question in chapter 4 as we study integration into the community.

The Family/Boarding Home Continuum

Homes can be seen along a continuum ranging from the equivalent of a boarding home to a home that is warm and familistic. As described by the interviewers, the homes that follow are representative of the boarding home end of the continuum. Note the wide range in the ages of the providers and the varying ages and abilities of the residents.

• Mrs. S., aged 54, lives with her husband and children. The residents are three men, aged 59 (retarded), 75, and 87, and a woman, aged 75. They have lived there between three months and two years. The oldest man previously lived in his own home; the other three came from an institution. The residents eat together, but not with the family. The residents rarely converse with each other or take part in group·projects. They may see former residents at the hospital, but it is not intentional. Residents only view each other as someone they live with, and don't interact with each other. There are birthday parties for the residents, but "some don't remember it's their birthday, even when the cake is in front of them." The interviewer commented: "Mr. and Mrs. S. took part in the interview.

Mr. S. was disgusted with the residents. 'All they do is sit around all day.' Mrs. S. attempted to get the residents to play bingo and do crafts when they started the home. It didn't work well, so she seems to have given up on doing anything. They complained that it was depressing seeing the residents especially on a snowy day, when they couldn't go out.

Mr. S. seemed to see the home as a business; Mrs. S. seemed a little more concerned about the residents and even had a few warm anecdotes about them."

- Mrs. T. is 58 and lives with her husband, who is employed part-time. There is a big shrine outside the house. The four women residents are aged 93, 83, 81, and 79. Five of the previous residents went back to their own homes. The interviewer commented: "I didn't get a terribly warm feeling from Mrs. T. When Mr. T. came in, he joked with the residents. Mrs. T. seemed more concerned with the regulations than with the residents. She talked in terms of feeding them good food so she felt her home was good. She says she goes out of her way to 'do good by them,' e.g., special St. Patrick's candy or cookies. Mrs. T. feels the elderly should be taken care of by relatives or in small homes like hers. Perhaps she isn't a very warm person because she said she'd take care of her relatives like the residents she has."

- Mrs. B. is 67 and lives with her husband. She has been in the community for over twenty years, and with the program for four years. The home had been a convalescent home for twenty five years, and became a Family-Type Home for Adults four years ago. There are three female residents aged 67–85, and one aged 46 who has been there only a month. The residents keep to themselves, doing things in their own rooms, such as reading the paper, listening to their own radios, looking out the windows, and praying. According to Mrs. B., one resident is slightly retarded and can't form friendships, one resident is a loner, and two residents have become friends with each other and visit with each other. Mrs. B. visits with each one. The day before the interview, one had a visit from relatives. Two residents have weekly visits from friends or relatives, and the other two have monthly visits. Two never go out to visit friends or relatives, and two rarely do. The residents very seldom participate with the family in outside activities; sometimes they go out in the yard. They haven't met the neighbors. The rewards of being a care provider include "keeping busy and active, and in contact with people." The disadvantages include "being tied down twenty four hours a day, and not making enough money with only four residents." The interviewer commented: "Mrs. B. seems to run this place as if it were a boarding house, or even a nursing home. Meals are served on trays, and the residents eat alone in their rooms. The residents seem to stay in their individual rooms all day. I didn't see any of them; they were all upstairs. Even though Mrs. B. claims they are all one big family, I have my doubts."

- Ms. M., aged 46, is blind, can't talk, and can't hear. The provider seems to feel responsible only for feeding her, dressing her, and making sure she's not left alone. Otherwise, she doesn't bother with her. She doesn't know when her birthday is. She "could find out, but why bother?" It is important to keep in mind that in the third study there were a number of nonverbal clients.

- Schoolteachers rent an apartment on the third floor of this family care home. The residents, aged 91, 85, and 87, are all widowed women. There are no other family members in the home. Mrs. K. has been in the program for four years, and has lived in the community for more than twenty years. She views the residents as boarders and friends. "These are three people who need help and I'm here to give them what service I can. It's very important to tell the (natural) family the residents are senile. Establish rules and regulations, to let them know. I'm kind, but I'm stern." The satisfactions of being a provider are "the compliments of the community, satisfaction of their families, the vast interest that doctors take, a lot of community support." The interviewer commented: "Mrs. K. remarked that maybe she has a bug about it but she thinks cleanliness is half of it. She was very proud of how clean her house was and was pleased to show me around. The residents' accommodations were very nice. 'All the residents get a full tub bath every week,' she told me, and winked for emphasis. She told me that she has a reputation in the community for being firm but kind, running a clean house and serving good food. My previous interview with a neighboring provider confirms the 'firm' in Mrs. K.'s self-description. I'm sure she cared about the residents, but it was not a family."

- Mrs. T., aged 70, married, has two residents, aged 72 and "about 60." The residents live in the downstairs apartment. She was going to rent out the apartment, but a friend who was a provider suggested family care, as being better than having people in and out of an apartment. According to the interviewer: "Mrs. T. didn't know very much about the residents. She spends most of her time upstairs; I think her husband is sick."

- Mrs. R., a widow, would not give her age, other than 60 plus; the interviewer suspects she is much older. The residents are three men, all in their 60s—Mrs. R. did not know their ages. They have lived with Mrs. R. for six years, four years, and six months. Two came from an institution, the third from another family care home. Mrs. R. has been with the program for twenty years. Mrs. R.'s husband had died and her son was at home. When her son was killed and she needed companionship, the undertaker suggested going to the psychiatric center to find residents. When Mrs. R. "bumps into former residents, or they come back to visit, I tell them to stay where they're living." Mrs. R. likes the residents but she is not too close with them. "The social worker tells us not to get too close." The rewards include "someone in the house with you." The interviewer commented: "I couldn't get out of there fast enough. House is a cross between a furniture store and a funeral parlor. Mrs. R. is a rickety old woman who seemed to doze off in the middle of her answers, but even when she was awake, she didn't know too much."

While care providing skills may be inherent in some of the providers, it is clear that training would probably have increased the ratings.

The next seven illustrative homes represent the familistic end of the continuum. Note that providers and residents have demographic characteristics similar to those just described. The homes differ only in their familism ratings.

- Mrs. A, a 76-year-old widow, has lived in the community for more than twenty years. She has been a provider for eight months and has two residents, aged 89 and 90. Both residents are "senile," but talk to each other. One resident had previously lived with a sister; after the sister died, the resident remained in the house with her sister for a few days until they were discovered. The resident and her dog were brought to Mrs. A. in an ambulance. The residents exchange gifts, but they are "too old" for outside activities like senior citizens clubs or crafts. The residents can't do chores, and they get upset when they go out to visit friends or relatives. They love to ride in the car. Mrs. A. prefers to take only women residents, because "the community talks about widows having men living in the home." Mrs. A. commented: "We are a family." The residents call her Nana. The interviewer commented: "The residents are part of a warm, extended family." (The majority of the neighbors are related.) Mrs. A.'s great-grandchildren come around to talk and help out with the residents. If she needs to be away, other family members take over. When asked about the rewards of being a care provider, Mrs. A. responded: "Doing for your fellow man, making older persons happy. When they kiss you good night, what more can you ask?"

- The three residents of this OMR home, men and women, are aged 56, 63, and 69. The provider, a 64-year-old widow, emphasized the feelings of family: "These residents are my family as much as my own flesh and blood are." The provider has no one else living with her. She has been with the program for eleven years; the sampled resident, Ms. H., aged 63, has been in the home for seven years. The provider commented: "Her sisters want to lock her up, so I only let them visit with the social worker present, because they treat Ms. H. so terribly. They laugh at her, threaten her, take her clothes off, etc." Ms. H. is friends with the grown children of the provider living in the neighborhood, and they eat together in restaurants. Ms. H. volunteers to do favors, but she is unable to. The provider commented: "When we're at the family camp, the campers will treat her to ice cream. All the campers know her and keep an eye on her. Ms. H. is too loud in church and the people don't like it, so now a priest comes to my home."

- The provider is a widow, aged 72, and has no other relatives living with her. There are two family care residents, both women, aged 44 and 50. The provider takes her residents traveling. They go to Florida or North Carolina and Cape Cod every year. The provider would like to adopt Ms. D. (aged 50 and nonverbal), but she feels too old.

- In the interviewer's words: "This was truly a family situation. A remarkably warm, loving lady." The provider, Mrs. B., is 37 years old and lives with her husband and children. Mr. C., the family care resident, is 64 years old and deaf and retarded. Mr. C. used to board with Mrs. B.'s mother, and then lived at the state hospital. Then, according to Mrs. B.: "He begged me to take him home, so I did" (five and a half years ago). He knew the neighbors because he had always lived in the community, and now he spends a lot of time with them. All rooms in the home are shared, and Mr. C. has kitchen privileges and helps with the chores. He always eats with the family, and only eats alone if Mrs. B. is working and he feels like eating. He goes with the family on vacation to their cottage. They exchange gifts as often as other family members do.

- Mrs. S. is a 67-year-old widow, who was formerly an innkeeper. She has been with the program for thirteen months. She has two residents, aged 72 and 65. Both women came from another family care home. All three eat together. They don't play cards or games with each other because they are "on the go too much." The residents go everywhere with Mrs. S., e.g., to visit her family, out to dinner, on rides, to the beauty shop, on a vacation to Florida. The interviewer commented: "This lady was great—A real down-to-earth person who, after her husband died, needed an income supplement and joined the program. However, even though she went into it for money, because she is such a decent person, she probably runs one of the best family care homes around."

• Mrs. N., aged 42 lives with her husband and children. She is a waitress four nights a week. "That's my out." She has been with the program for eight years. The two residents are women, aged 63 and 60. They have each been there for about seven years. The first came from an institution, and the other from another family care home. The interviewer commented: "This house was a real family. People 'milling about,' kids on Mrs. N.'s lap, Mrs. N. combing one resident's hair, people drifting in and out of the family room to watch TV." All meals are eaten together. The residents go wherever Mrs. N. goes, e.g., shopping, out for lunch, to camp. They all do housework and gardening together. She views her relationship with the residents as family, and never likes to refer to them as patients. If residents arrive without suitable clothing, Mrs. N. buys what they need, to give to them on Christmas and birthdays. If a resident creates a problem, "we just fight it out like any other family does."

• Mrs. V. is 50 years old and lives with her spouse and daughter. The four residents are aged 79, 64, and two younger than 60. One previously lived in an institution, and the other in another family care home. Mrs. V. commented: "When my husband was ill, the residents were very worried about him. They feel what we feel. I think they really crave affection and they respond to affection. Even as old as they are, they still grow." One resident (Mrs. T.) goes across the street to visit a former family care provider who is now too old to have residents. Mrs. T. visits with her every day and makes sure everything is OK with her. When asked how she handles problems with the residents, Mrs. V. responded: "I cope with it the way I would with my own family. I try not to chastise them in front of each other." Mrs. V. suggested that there should be a family care program for people who are not mentally ill. The interviewer commented: "I met the residents. They are very well groomed and demonstrative toward Mrs. V. Really a nice place. Residents were very friendly and talkative. Mrs. V. showed me a Mother's Day card she had received from one resident and pointed it out to me in front of her. Mrs. V. commented how proud of this she was. The resident was all ears and basking in appreciation."

In contrast to the impersonal flavor of the first set of homes, for some respondents providing a home for frail older persons gave a great deal of personal satisfaction. Foster family care might, therefore, be used more extensively as a benefit to the provider, particularly if she herself is elderly. A "traditional" family may not be necessary in a foster home. More family-type interaction may actually occur between resident and provider when fewer "natural" family members are present. Being a family care provider might provide persons who are themselves in their fifties and older and who have no natural family of their own on the premises with a meaningful role in their later years. This might be particularly important for widows.

Attachment and Dependency

The provider and the resident sometimes can be seen in reciprocal roles, each fulfilling her needs for adult attachment (Bowlby 1969; Sable 1979). Some of these needs are the needs for affiliation, expressing emotion, and having these emotions responded to. Adult affective or expressive needs must be distinguished from unhealthy dependency needs whose reciprocal role is that of control. A healthy approach to fulfillment of the former is similar to that sought in some other small housing alternatives, such as shared housing. The following vignettes illustrate attachment roles that are typical in family care.

• Mrs. D. is a 69-year-old widow, in a wheelchair. Her grandson, aged 25, lives with her. The family care residents include four women, aged 49 through 64. Two of the residents have been with her for fifteen years. Previously, all four lived in institutions. Mrs. D. has been with the program for twenty five years. She had foster children, and her doctor's wife suggested she get involved with the "girls" at the institution. Mrs. D. plays cards with the residents every night, and they all eat together. The residents work together on housework. Mrs. D. commented: "Some homes are like an institution, large tables, set times to do everything. . . . Here the girls are in a family." When asked the rewards of being a provider, Mrs. D. answered: "We each put a roof over each other's heads. Giving people a home until they can get on their own. I help the residents; the residents help me." The interviewer commented: "Seemed like real family. Kidding back and forth. The resident who's been there less than a week seems like she's been there forever. Mrs. D. started to cry when she told me about a former resident who died."

• Mrs. E., a 55-year-old widow, has three family care residents, aged 82, 61, and 52. The interviewer commented: "She's a widow and they really are company for her, particularly the 82-year-old who was in the hospital for forty years before she came here. She's been with Mrs. E. for five and a half years. Mrs. E. gave her a beautiful corsage for Mother's Day, and Mrs. E.'s daughter gave her a lovely purse." Mrs. E. and the residents go everywhere together: camping, across the street to the neighbor's for coffee. When asked why she became involved in the program, Mrs. E. commented: "Prevents being all alone. My husband is dead, and my daughter is out of town." The rewards include "gratification when you get discharges; very good company, just like my own sister."

On the other hand, Mrs. J., a 66-year-old widow, does not seem to need the residents for her family.

• At present, Mrs. J. has four residents aged 68, 31, 46, and 41, all female, all retarded. They previously were at a state school. Also in the house are Mrs. J.'s grandchild, daughter, and her 88-year-old mother. Mrs. J. has lived in the community for over five years. She views the residents as "boarders." According to the interviewer, "Mrs. J. feels having a clean house is important. The residents probably get very good care. It may even feel like family to the residents, as Mrs. J. said, but Mrs. J. is not part of that family. She's more like a strict housemother, I would think. If any of the residents are accepted into the fringes of Mrs. J.'s family, it is the elderly resident. The younger ones have their own group. This lady has ten children, many siblings, mother, forty four grandchildren. She doesn't need any more family."

Person-Environment Congruence in Family Care

Finally, some cases can be described as good examples of person-environment congruence.

• Mrs. N., aged 40, lives with her husband and children. The resident, Mrs. O., was in the room during the entire interview and indicated that she was happy with her situation. Mrs. O., an 82-year-old widow, was in poor physical condition (incontinent) and could not speak well, yet this was "OK" with Mrs. N. because she had worked as a nurse's aide in a nursing home and knew how to take care of such persons. The interviewer commented: "I felt that this particular resident was fortunate in having found somebody willing not only to take care of her, but to accept her into the family as well. Also, the children seemed especially well adjusted to her presence. Mrs. O. is usually in the living room, and the kids sing and entertain her most of the time."

• Mrs. C. is 41 and lives in a rural area with her husband and children. Her residents are an 89-year-old woman and two men, aged 88 and 90. The 90-year-old is just placed temporarily, while his family is on vacation for three weeks. All the residents have come from the community. Mrs. C. has been in the program for just over a year, and has had eight previous residents, most for only two or three months. The interviewer commented: "This was one of the best homes I have seen. This lady has taken in people who really need a great deal of care, yet she seems more than willing to do everything she can for them. I met all three residents (Mrs. R. and Mrs. C. even sang a song for me), and even though the residents are in poor physical and mental condition, they seem to enjoy Mrs. C. and their surroundings very much." This home received a very high familism rating.

• Mrs. H., aged 54, and her husband are both RNs; therefore, the hospital sends people who need temporary skilled observation (regarding diets, injections, etc.). At the present time there are four residents, aged 85–91. Mrs. H. has been in C—for three years and had a home for adults for up to eight residents in M—for seventeen years. There also is a 25-year-old family friend living there, and Mrs. H.'s son has the attic apartment when he's home from school. According to the interviewer, "Mrs. H. speaks of the residents with a tremendous amount of affection. Her eyes often fill up as she talks. Mention of the possibility of the death of one of the residents caused her considerable distress. While I was there one of the residents had to go to the doctor's. There was a lot of scurrying around over who would take her or should she get a cab and who would pick her up and where were the keys to the car, etc. Very familial atmosphere. Mr. H. was making jokes with a resident and the resident was sticking her tongue out at Mr. H. Visitors in and out and phone ringing and so on." Mrs. H. commented: "They should make us a skilled facility, or increase the rate for us. We can't afford to take SSI [supplemental security income] people because of the rate we get, but if they would give us a higher rate we would. The state restrictions annoy me. I can understand the state's position, but they are forcing homes like ours out and making them less and less personal. People like us, who enjoy doing this, will be pushed out and it will be a loss."

It appears that these homes can fulfill the needs well for a particular segment of the population, a population that will continue to grow: the frail elderly. The providers frequently have background experience to deal with persons with physical impairments, and indeed are quite nurturant. Second, many of the homes provide continuity with the previous lives of the residents. Third, the environment permits individual treatment and tolerance for deviance. We have many instances of the characteristics of the environment suggested in Kahana's (1982) model of person-environment congruence. It appeared that in most cases the level of affection, social interaction, social distance, and ritual found in these homes fit the needs of both the providers and the residents. With clarification of what is expected by familism and training so that residents and providers are better able to understand and adapt to their new roles, foster homes can, indeed, be viewed as foster "family" homes.

Summary: In this chapter we have explored the extent to which the resident actually does become a part of the family. We described the development of a scale to measure the concept of familism, based on program documents, literature pertaining to adult foster family care, and sociological theory about families. The various measures of familism, designed to include the four dimensions of affection, social interaction, social distance, and ritual indicated that family integration and participation do occur in these foster family homes for adults. Although there was great diversity across indicators, and from study to study, it was concluded that familism, as defined in the present study, was present in about two-thirds of the homes. The evidence indicated that the relationship between provider and resident was more frequently perceived as familial than that which existed among the residents themselves. The chapter concluded with themes central to the family care model: the co-existence of rules with informality and flexibility; challenge in the environment; the family-boarding home continuum; attachment and dependency; and person-environment congruence.

4 · Community Integration of Residents of Foster Family Care

Chapter 1 reviewed the rationale for placement in the community of various dependent populations of older persons. Thus, alternatives to nursing homes have been sought for the elderly in the expectation that not only financial benefits but psychological benefits will accrue if the person is in a more natural environment. Programs such as home care, day care, and respite have emerged. Frequently, however, the person is too frail to remain in his/her own home and needs some sort of support. Foster family care is a possible alternative, although it has not been used extensively for elderly persons who are merely frail rather than mentally ill or mentally retarded. Foster care must build upon the use of community resources. The New York State Board of Social Welfare, for example, required that "if they so desire, guests shall be permitted and assisted to maintain their place in community life" (State of New York, BSW, undated: 4).

The community mental health movement also prescribes building on both formal and informal supports in the community. Deinstitutionalization during the past twenty years or so has put thousands back into the community, either those released from institutions or those who might have been institutionalized but are instead left in the community. Since many deinstitutionalized persons do not have "natural" families, alternative residences, including foster family care, must be found. Departmental regulations expect that there will be participation in activities outside the home.

In the field of mental retardation/developmental disabilities, placing clients in the community rather than in institutions is part of the philosophy of normalization. Again, foster family care is one alternative and tends to be used disproportionately by the elderly (Bruininks, Hill, and Thorsheim 1982). For all three groups, the frail elderly, the mentally ill, and the developmentally disabled, merely taking one's meals and sleeping in a private home in the community are not, however, sufficient. It is fair to judge that the disabled person has not truly been returned to the community if she spends her time in isolation, whether living alone, in a hotel, or even in foster family care. Development is enhanced for some by participation in a variety of settings (Bronfenbrenner 1979).

Murphy, Pennee, and Luchins (1972) reported very little transaction with the community outside the homes on the part of the schizophrenic patients (not primarily geriatric or "deficient") living in larger foster homes. Murphy and his colleagues attributed this to geographic distance, lack of funds, having clothes and haircuts marking them as "ex-patients," feelings of not being welcome, and most important, an absence of reaching out by community members. There was almost no participation in community groups. There was not even any social exchange with neighbors other than the simple exchange of greetings as they passed each other outside. At least a minimum level of transaction with the community is expected to distinguish such community living from life in an institution. As described by Aviram and Segal, "Physical inclusion is a necessary, but not a sufficient condition for the integration of the mentally ill in the community. The question of social exclusion . . . is in much need of research" (1973: 130). Cohen and Kligler (1980) claim that the living arrangements per se should not be defined as normalization, but rather as providing a "home base" for normalization. Similarly, Intagliata, Crosby, and Neider assert that "an important aspect of normalized life in the community is the degree to which mentally retarded persons make use of a variety of community resources frequented by others" (1981: 243).

In family care the intent is for the residents to use community resources, including social and recreation programs, pharmacies, and physicians. For example, OMR policy is for providers to arrange for and encourage "clients to participate in periodic recreational, cultural, and social activities in the community according to each client's abilities" (State of New York, OMR, 1986: 10.6.2 [rev.], p. 1). When placing patients in family care, the facility personnel evaluate the accessibility of the home to such resources and to transportation for mobility and involvement. However, Bradshaw et al. (1975) noted that, in spite of its potential benefits, foster family care as an attempt at community integration has received relatively little systematic study. Studies of community integration of the mentally ill have for the most part neither investigated family care as an alternative in the continuum of care, nor compared the use of community alternatives across different age groups. Additionally, those few studies that have been conducted on foster family care have not emphasized community integration as an outcome measure. If community integration is conceptualized as permeability, the most permeable setting is one that encourages interaction between family care residents and other community members.

COMMUNITY RESISTANCE TO ALTERNATE FORMS OF CARE

Although in some communities there has been resistance to congregate housing (Butler 1969; Lawton and Hoffman 1984; Mangum 1985a, 1985b), there has not been as much resistance to community alternatives for the elderly as there has been to alternatives for other groups, such as the mentally ill and mentally retarded. In fact, Mangum (1985a) reports that when there was opposition to congregate housing for the elderly, opponents denied that negativism toward the elderly per se was a motivation. He also reports (1985b) that group housing for the elderly (a cluster of single-story apartments, a large older home housing five to ten unrelated persons, and a multistory apartment building) was perceived as less objectionable in the respondents single-family neighborhoods than as group housing for the mentally retarded or for former patients of state mental hospitals, which in turn was less objectionable than group housing for male juvenile delinquents.

Unfortunately, there has been a great deal of resistance to current and former mental patients and mentally retarded persons in the community (Baker, Seltzer, and Seltzer 1974; Cocozza and Steadman 1976; O'Connor 1976; Savasta 1979). There is a great deal of literature attributing the failure of community integration among former patients to community opposition, stigmatization, and nontolerance of deviance (Schulberg, Becker, and McGrath 1976; Wolpert, Dear, and Crawford 1975). Aviram and Segal (1973) refer to the development of both formal and informal systems of exclusion. There have been newspaper campaigns, petitions, zoning changes, and other pressures to keep such persons out of communities. Indeed, nonacceptance by the community has often been cited as a major cause of the failure of community placements (Bruininks, Hill, and Thorsheim 1982; Gollay 1976; Justice, Bradley, and O'Connor 1971; Morrissey 1966; Tinsley, O'Connor, and Halpern 1973).

There is a body of evidence, however, indicating that opposition to a facility tends to decline over time after the facility has opened (Lauber and Bangs 1974; Mangum 1985a; O'Connor 1976). Miller (1977) found that complaints about the VA program he studied were so infrequent that a file had not even been established. Thus, based on conflicting evidence, the degree of acceptance by the community is still largely unknown.

Mangum suggests that any type of group housing, regardless of the age or other characteristics of the residents, is likely to be opposed in "communities that consist primarily of single family homes" (1985a: 11), for fear of changing the neighborhood character (1985b). One question addressed by our study is the extent to which resistance generalizes to small foster family care settings. Perhaps the fact that the care provider is a community member herself makes the way easier for the residents. The provider offers built-in links between the family care setting and other settings, thus increasing the developmental potential of the setting (Bronfenbrenner 1979). Additionally, since one of the sources of negative reaction to mental patients in the community is fear that patients are dangerous and unpredictable, agencies have expressed the expectation that not only will the individual client benefit from community placement, but over time the presence of such persons will diminish fear and increase the community's tolerance (State of New York, Department of Mental Hygiene 1974).

In addition to the community's acceptance or rejection of the family care program and its participants, participation in the affairs of the community is dependent upon several factors: the client's capability and willingness to participate, the family's encouragement, and the accessibility of the home. In a study of a VA Community Care Program, although social relationships in the foster care homes were primarily limited to interactions between providers and residents, Miller (1977) found that some residents did participate in social and cultural activities in town. Although providers were encouraged to help residents to use recreation available in the community, the staff perceived a lack of community resources and difficulty in motivating residents to engage in social activities. For example, in rural areas homes may be less visible, but if too hidden, they may not provide the residents with the opportunity to participate in the ongoing life of the community. Conversely, persons who are "different" might be more obvious in rural or suburban areas than in an anonymous urban area. Our studies have tested to what extent foster family care is associated with normalization, that is, penetration into the community, and the importance of client, provider, and home characteristics in facilitating or inhibiting integration.

TWO ASPECTS OF COMMUNITY INTEGRATION: ACCEPTANCE AND PARTICIPATION

Community integration can be viewed in terms of two levels of integration. The first, a necessary but perhaps not sufficient component, is *acceptance* of the residents by neighbors and other community members. Beyond this is a more active *participation* by residents in the life of the community and interaction with its members. Only if some participation takes place can we say that a resident has truly penetrated into the community.

In our studies we investigated whether there was resistance by the community to the clients. Since other members of the community were not interviewed, community response can only be discussed as it is perceived and interpreted by the caretakers and, in our second study, the residents. A number of separate indicators of community acceptance were measured and will be presented one at a time. Next, two sum scores are described, each of which combines several single-item indicators of acceptance. The first of these sum scores is used later in the chapter as an outcome measure when determining which client, home, and care provider characteristics predict community acceptance.

In addition to community acceptance, we investigated community participation. To what extent does the resident use the resources of the community, such as shops, barbers, and drugstores? To what extent does the resident interact with neighbors, relatives, and friends inthe community, and to what extent does the resident engage in generic activities in the community, such as movies, concerts, sports events? These also were used as outcome measures with client, home, and provider characteristics as predictors.

Community Acceptance

Conceptually, community acceptance means that the residents are treated in the community just like other residents. In some cases this merely means being left alone, with the resident spending most of the time in the family care residence or in other settings, such as special programs for the disabled. In other instances this means that the neighbors engage in conversations with the residents, or that residents are welcomed into neighbors' homes. Betts, Moore, and Reynolds (1981) suggested that welcoming friends and neighbors into the home and avoiding deviant labels are two criteria for normalization in boarding homes for chronic mentally ill patients. It means that neighbors and other community residents do not stare at the residents when they venture out into the community or single them out for differential treatment, e.g., exclude them from senior centers. For example, Mrs. T., a DSS provider (first study) with two residents from a psychiatric center, commented that some of the neighbors "don't really understand the residents; that is one reason why the residents don't go to the senior citizens center. The members won't accept them. This happens with church also."

In order to understand fully community resistance to residents of foster family care, it is essential first to assess whether residents are identified as "special," for example, as mental patients, or whether they blend into the community. As reported in chapter 2, with respect to behavioral ratings, only 5 percent were described by providers as often or always exhibiting strange behavior in public, or hostile behavior that could be perceived by the community as threatening. Interviewers reported that for about half the OMH residents, "having seen him or her in any other place I would not think there was anything unusual about him or her." Another one-third judged that the "resident looks a little different but not disturbingly so," and the remainder (13 percent) judged that the "resident looks disturbingly different." Residents were asked whether people in the community recognized them as former psychiatric patients. About three-quarters of the residents felt that at least some of the people in the neighborhood knew of their hospitalization.

Despite any specific "image" attributed to the homes, as shown in tables 4.1, and 4.2, the response to both the idea of having a foster home for adults in the neighborhood and to specific residents was generally favorable. The incidence of disapproval was extremely low. A favorable response was given across all three populations of foster home residents, and was perceived by both providers and residents. Providers were also asked how people respond when the specific resident appears in a public place like church or local shops. Responses were similar to those given for neighbors' attitudes: in

Table 4.1
Perception of Neighbors' Response to Having Foster Home for Adults in Neighborhood (%)

	DSS	DMH	OMH
(N)	(50)	(50)	(99)
General approval/very favorable	48	66	49
Somewhat favorable	—	—	27
Don't care/neutral	46	24	24
Providers don't know	2	4	—
Some approve, others do not	2	6	—
General disapproval/unfavorable	2	0	0

Note: Question was not asked in study 3. In study 1, response alternatives were general approval, don't seem to care, respondents don't know, some approve, others do not, and general disapproval. In study 2, response alternatives were very favorable, somewhat favorable, neutral, somewhat unfavorable, and very unfavorable.

study 2 (OMH) 19 percent reported "warm and accepting" and 76 percent reported "generally friendly"; in study 3 (OMR) 15 percent reported "warm and accepting" and 56 percent reported "generally friendly." It is of interest to focus more specifically on positive and negative incidents that providers and residents encountered from neighbors. Nearly half the OMH and OMR providers (41 and 48 percent, respectively) reported positive or favorable incidents experienced by the residents, such as meeting with general friendliness, receiving cards, gifts, and food, getting rides downtown and home, exchanging favors by neighbors and family care residents, and being invited to birthday parties, craft groups, and to go bike riding.

Favorable comments included the following: Miss X.'s appearance "looks better," Ms. C. (a 64-year-old woman) is "cute," Ms. M. (aged 51) has a neat, clean appearance, and Ms. S. (aged 53) and the other residents are "a wonderful bunch of girls, e.g., they do errands." (The first of these residents was in the Mental Hygiene system; the other three were from OMR.) Another resident's neighbors commented on her knitting skills. These comments would seem to represent a rather minimal level of acceptance, however.

The area's dependence on the psychiatric center and its clients was indicated in several OMH interviews. This results in an ambivalence: community attitudes might be negative on an individual basis, but at the same time the townspeople realize the economic benefits they derive from the clients. For example, one provider

Table 4.2
Neighbors' Response to Specific Resident (%)

	Care Provider's Perception		Resident's Perception
	OMH	OMR	OMH
(N)	(99)	(148)	(86)
Warm and accepting	25	39	15
Generally friendly	69	46	66
Indifferent	3	6	9
Avoids resident	0	2	1
Hostile, annoyed	0	0	0
Mixed or other	3	7	9

Note: Neither question was asked in study 1. Second question was not asked in study 3.

reported that her resident, a 30-year-old man, uses the neighbor's pool. She continued: "Everybody is nice to all the men [residents] here all the time. This is because of the dependence of the town on the psychiatric center and how nice 'my men' are. The town needs the jobs from the psychiatric center and people have accepted this. It's been there forever. The neighbors are all really good to these people."

The residents themselves were asked to report positive or favorable incidents with the neighbors. Again, some of the interactions included invitations: "They let me visit and smoke in their house." "We play cards, have nice social times, drink ginger ale, and listen to the radio." I was invited to a birthday party by Mrs. L.'s [the provider] sister-in-law." "Two different neighbors invited me to a bridal shower and weddings."

One of the residents alluded to a process whereby the neighbors, who had known him before when he previously lived in the neighborhood, seemed to become used to him. It was not possible to ascertain the role the provider played in this process of assimilation: "When I first came back from the hospital, the people I knew were mean to me, but they have been nice for a long time. I've been invited into my neighbor's homes often. The neighbors are completely nice."

Positive comments and an exchange of greetings were also reported by the residents: "There is a man on the street who goes to Bible study. I speak to him, we exchange greetings." "I talk to the lady walking her dog. I go to McDonalds every day for coffee and visit with the people there even though I don't know their names." "I am friends with the storekeepers on a first-name basis." "Many people speak to me on the street, even children." "I meet the neighbors at the mall and we're friendly." (In this case the interviewer commented that she saw a general picture of exchanging greetings with neighbors but not much more interaction. For example, the resident goes to library, post office, or shopping mall often by herself or with other residents.)

Favors were given or granted: "A neighbor accepted some books for me. Another neighbor loaned me money once. He trusted me and I paid back the money." "One of the neighbors brings over dinner if Mrs. J. [the provider] is asked out." "A couple times I used the neighbor's clothesline." "I've helped neighbors in trouble. For example, when one woman's drapes fell down, I helped put them up." "The neighbors will sometimes offer me rides home when I'm out walking." "I do odd jobs once a week for the next-door neighbor. I got a reward for telling some kids that their bikes were stolen and helping them get them back."

Finally, some comments reflected the residents' ambivalence, or approach-avoidance conflict with regard to neighbors: "I had dinner at church, that was pleasant. I also had dinner at the fire hall. Everyone from the village attended. The neighbors walk with me and they speak nice. Or if I got something new on they compliment me. I don't think it's nice to impose on the neighbors. They have their families." "When the neighbors come to visit Mrs. R. [the provider] they say hello. I walk away. I keep to myself. It's better that way. You get along better."

Negative incidents were reported by about 13 percent of the providers—much less frequently than positive incidents. Problems included rumors, petitions, complaints about behavior. "A few neighbors fought to stop having mental patients in the community." There were also indications that the problems had been resolved: "The neighbors tried to close me down and gave bad reports to DSS. I had to get a lawyer. Then I had an open house and no one showed up." "A few neighbors resisted having a family care home in 1972 when I started, and I needed to gather signatures in order to start the home. Neighbors are very positive now."

Some of the behavior problems indicated that the residents had been placed inappropriately or prematurely. "There was a complaint about him staring at the young girls." "Years ago there was a complaint about a man begging." "When she went to the grocery, she created a scene, started screaming, knocking over displays. When she appears in public places, people stare at her, but don't really avoid her or act mean." "Most people tell him to be quiet because he talks too much. The neighbors all keep an eye on him for me. There was a negative incident at a picnic: he went to the bathroom on a tree and shocked everyone."

There was some attempt on the part of the providers to keep the residents away from trouble: "When I first opened the home ten years ago, a neighbor complained. One of the male residents had shaken hands with her little girl. I told the resident not to speak to people around here unless spoken to. There haven't been any complaints since then." In another home, according to the interviewer, "Mrs. A. [provider] kept saying everything was fine there, but she also kept stressing that she didn't let her 'girls' bother anyone, not everyone likes handicapped people, etc. Mrs. A. seems very aware that her girls are 'different.'" Another provider commented, "He can't converse too well so it makes it hard to interact with neighbors. I guard him and prevent negative incidents. He does tend to be aggressive and could turn people off."

Only a few negative incidents were reported by residents: "A child pointed a finger and said I was a bum." One wonders if this was a comment the child had heard from his or her parents. "A neighbor said to me that she didn't like family care people living in the neighborhood." An unexpected response indicated overreaction on the part of the neighbors: "I slipped on the ice and people in the area called the police."

In the second study (OMH) we asked the residents directly about their satisfaction with their relationship with the neighbors. Nearly all (96 percent) stated that they were satisfied. A few said they would like to get to know their neighbors better. However, about half said they did not have much in common with their neighbors. Of course, we should keep in mind that many persons who are not disabled in any way consider that they have little in common with their neighbors. About one-quarter said it was difficult to meet neighbors because "it's my nature; I don't open up easily or mix too much."

A couple of residents in the OMH study reported being discouraged from mixing by the provider. "It has been difficult to meet neighbors because the family care lady wants me not to tell anyone my business; she'd rather that I mind my own business more." (Probe: She'd rather you not talk to the neighbors?) "Yes, she would." The interviewer commented that no anger was shown while saying this. In another home, the resident stated that "Mrs. Y. doesn't want me to visit the neighbors or her daughter next door, but her daughter invites us, so I go and really enjoy short visits." The provider's view of this was different: "My neighbor told Mrs. T. [the resident] to come less often to visit. She had gone to one neighbor every day, and the neighbor told her to come once a week."

There can be advantages of a concentration of family care residents. In some communities, there is more than one family care home on the block. Even if they penetrate no farther into the community, this enables the residents at least to leave the shelter of their own home and get together with the residents from the other homes. For example, in one home it was reported that the residents go to a local shopping mall where many family care residents shop. Often the psychiatric center employees go there also, so the residents are able to have quite a bit of continuity. On the other hand, in the third study 55 percent of the clients lived in homes where no other residential facilities or family care homes for disabled persons were located within a radius of four blocks. This could result in less visibility and perhaps more community acceptance, at least of a passive nature.

In order to have more stable outcome measures, in the second study a factor analysis was performed on fifty-nine items relating to community integration. One factor emerged containing items that pertained to community acceptance. The items measured penetration into the neighborhood, from the resident's viewpoint. We labeled the factor neighbor acceptance scale, and items appear in table 4.3. The providers were asked about these same items in the third study. One of the items had been asked about in the first study. The ordering of the responses was remarkably similar across populations (especially considering that we have the residents' report in one study and the providers' report in the other two). In each study we find a wide range of responses across items with at least three-fourths of the residents having met the neighbors, but only one-third to one-half reporting invitations to neighbors' homes or having friends in the neighborhood. These last two indicators require greater personal involvement.

A second scale, satisfaction with neighbors, was an adaptation of Bardo's (1976) community satisfaction measure. On five of the six items, OMH residents indicated a high level of satisfaction: "Almost everyone in this neighborhood or area is polite and courteous to me" (87 percent agree); "I feel very much at home in this neighborhood or area" (87 percent agree); "A lot of people in this neighborhood or area think they are too nice for me" (82 percent disagree); "You are out of luck in this neighborhood or area if you happen to be from a psychiatric center" (79 percent disagree); "People in this neighborhood or area give you a bad name if you are a little bit different" (76 percent disagree). On the sixth item, answers were about evenly distributed between positive and negative: "Real friends are hard to find in this neighborhood or area" (53 percent disagree). This suggests that the first five elements reflected casual acquaintances, whereas the sixth item indicated the absence of deeper relationships. This pattern is similar to that found on the previous factor, interaction with neighbors, and is consistent with a superficial level of community involvement. It appears that most of the items on the satisfaction scale represent passive tolerance as contrasted to active penetration. This contrast will become even more apparent when we discuss community participation.

In general, although many residents do not consider they have much in common with neighbors, and only a minority report significant intermingling, this is still a sizable minority. For the most

Table 4.3
Neighbor Acceptance Scale (%)

	DSS	DMH	OMH[a]	OMR
(N)	(127)	(99)	(95)	(151)
Met neighbors	76	85	73	93
Spent time with neighbors at least several times a year:[b]	—	—	45	—
With provider	—	—	—	76
Without provider	—	—	—	45
Experienced positive incidents	—	—	40	48
Was invited to neighbors' homes	—	—	36	50
Had friends in neighborhood	—	—	33	40
Neighbor acceptance mean sum score	—	—	(45.8)	(58.8)

Note: Only the first question was asked in study 1.
[a]Responses are those given by residents because they clustered on the factor analysis.
[b]In the third study providers were asked to distinguish between time spent with neighbors with and without the provider.

part, community acceptance is high. Despite hostility reported in the literature toward these populations, in our studies of foster family care, there have been few negative or hostile incidents. Resident satisfaction is high and there is general approval of the homes and the residents, with many examples of positive reactions from neighbors. We must consider, of course, whether receptivity in specific programs, e.g., senior citizens centers, is as high as general acceptance of the foster home in the neighborhood.

Community Participation

After assessing the degree to which residents are accepted by the community, we looked at the degree to which they actually participate in the life of the community. Three levels of penetration were studied. These included simply using community resources or services, socializing with familiar people, and participating in activities in the community. (Some of the items were adapted from Moos and Lemke's [1979] integration in the community scale.) According to Janicki, "Integration means that people are given the opportunity to move and communicate in age-appropriate ways, and to use typical community services, such as . . . stores . . . transportation, and health services" (1981:62). This type of integration, however, is rather passive, and may involve only minimal interaction with community members.

The next level of integration, socialization, reflects interaction with familiar persons in the informal network: relatives, friends, and neighbors. Although going to restaurants, churches, parks, etc., might be solitary pursuits, it was judged that participation in these activities requires a higher level of independence than socialization with familiar persons. Therefore, the most demanding level of integration is that in which the residents share and participate in the same activities as do other members of the community, such as using public places or attending social events.

Providers were asked what they did to encourage residents to spend time in the community. Their most common responses were that when they themselves went out they took the resident along, or that they transported the resident to psychiatric center activities, community resources, or visits. About two-thirds replied that they took the resident with them when they went shopping, to the movies, to restaurants, to church, or visiting. Nearly one-quarter reported that they introduced the resident to friends or neighbors. One provider reported: "I usually drive them to the bus stop or if the weather is bad I pick them up. Usually they don't take buses, I drive them. What's my life is their life. They don't do much on their own. If I go visiting or to the races or out to eat, I take them. They want me to go everywhere they go. My relatives accept them." On the other hand, one provider (an 82-year-old widow) without a car reported that "it's very hard for them to get out unless someone from the nearby institution volunteers to take them shopping."

Use of Community Resources. It is the policy of the psychiatric centers and developmental centers to further community integration through the encouragement of the use of community resources by the clients. Since the residents could in theory receive all the services of the community either through the psychiatric or developmental center (e.g., doctors) or through the providers in their homes (e.g., groceries), actual use of the resources in the community by the resident is an indicator of an attempt at integration.

Six community resources were identified and are listed in table 4.4. The highest usage was of barbers/hairdressers and doctors. The use of groceries, drugstores, and dentists was also high. Perhaps the lower use of community post offices can be explained by the

Table 4.4
Use of Community Resources (%)

	OMH	OMR
(N)	(97–101)	(150–151)
Barber	88	92
Doctor	82	95
Grocery	79	65
Drugstore	75	60
Dentist	63	76
Post office	52	38
Resources mean sum score	(73.3)	(70.9)

Note: Questions were not asked in study 1.

lower communication skills among these dependent groups, and by the unlikelihood of having friends at a distance with whom they might correspond. Despite the somewhat low use of one resource, on this level of participation, residents—both in OMH and OMR homes—appear to be penetrating into the community.

Socialization. After examining residents' use of services in the community, we can now look at their socialization with familiar members of their network. Does foster family care encourage their continued or increased interaction with friends, neighbors, and relatives, or does it cut people off from such contacts? Since our study did not include a longitudinal design, we cannot compare socialization before entry into the homes with socialization after. We can, however, compare socialization in the company of the provider with that without the provider. The latter can represent two types of social interaction—either the resident accompanies the provider as the latter socializes, or the provider accompanies the resident in an attempt to encourage the resident to reach out. Another point should be considered as well: neighbors may represent contacts brought about by foster family care if the resident has moved into a new neighborhood; relatives and possibly friends would have been available independent of foster family care. Therefore, there is a possibility that foster family care enhances socialization with neighbors while it reduces socialization with relatives.

Social network interaction is reported in table 4.5. More detailed breakdowns and resident responses for study 2 (OMH) can be found in Sherman, Frenkel, and Newman (1986). In the second and third studies sum scores were computed combining responses for friends, relatives, and neighbors, and these appear in the last rows of table 4.5. For the most part, the reported level of socialization was low, and became even lower if we used "at least once a month" as a cutoff. There were exceptions, however, such as the 40-year-old resident in OMH who appeared to be very integrated, according to the interviewer: "She has a part-time paid job five days a week. She has a boyfriend whom she sees often. She knows the neighbors. Most of these neighbors are relatives of the provider. She has been invited to their weddings."

Table 4.5 indicates that DSS clients had higher levels of socialization with friends and relatives, both in and out of the house, than did the DMH clients. Perhaps fewer ties had been broken in the lives of the former. Although the interview items were changed after the first study, the level of socialization with neighbors reported in study 1 (DSS/DMH) is similar to that reported in studies 2 (OMH) and 3 (OMR).

Some interesting comparisons between OMH and OMR residents were found in the level of socialization. First, we note that *without* the provider, OMH and OMR residents have approximately the same

Table 4.5
Socialization (%)

	DSS	DMH	OMH[a]	OMR[a]
(N)	(123–131)	(95–96)	(97–100)	(147–151)
Friends				
With provider[b]	86[c]	46[d]	19	79
Without provider[b]	73[e]	47[f]	28	36
Relatives				
With provider	(see	(see	10	18
Without provider	above	above)	43	19
Neighbors				
With provider	—	—	33	76
Without provider	—	—	30	45
Walks[g]	37	29	—	—
Visits[g]	40	55	—	—
Socialization mean sum score[h]				
With provider	—	—	(20.5)	(57.8)
Without provider	—	—	(34.1)	(33.2)

[a]Participation ranged from once a day to several times a year; once a year or less was considered nonparticipation.

[b]In the first study we did not distinguish between friends and relatives. Also, rather than distinguishing between with and without the provider, we asked, "About how often do your elderly residents have their friends or relatives visit at the house?" (first row in table) and "How often does each of the residents go outside of the house to visit friends or relatives?" (second row in table). Participation ranged from rarely to daily in the first case and from rarely to weekly in the second.

[c]If we exclude "rarely," 64% participated.

[d]If we exclude "rarely," 20% participated.

[e]If we exclude "rarely," 48% participated.

[f]If we exclude "rarely," 20% participated.

[g]In the first study we did not distinguish between socialization with and without the provider. We asked, "Do the residents take walks or visit with anyone in the neighborhood?"

[h]Not computed in the first study as items were not comparable.

level of socialization, overall. *With* the provider, the overall level is much higher for OMR than OMH. The fact that the difference between the two populations is so much greater with the provider than without the provider emphasizes the importance of the provider.

Second, when we take a more detailed look, we note, curiously, that the provider's presence makes a larger difference for the OMR residents than for the OMH residents, with respect to socialization with neighbors and friends. There is a different pattern with relatives: here, with the provider the OMH level of socialization is almost equal to OMR, but without the provider the level is higher for OMH residents than for OMR. As we will discuss in more detail in the next chapter, the OMH residents had more relatives nearby than did the OMR residents.

Third, for OMH residents the level of socialization with friends and relatives is higher without the provider than with the provider. All of these patterns are not easily explained, and need to be replicated in other studies.

Activities. The third type of community participation is that in which residents share and participate in the same activities as other members of the community. Stroud and Murphy (1984) found that most of the recreational activities for the older mentally retarded persons they studied were done as a group, supervised by the staff, and with little interaction with other members of the community. While it can be argued that going to restaurants, churches, parks, and so on might be done in isolation and involve no actual participation with others, it was judged that participation in these activities requires the ability to interact with strangers, perhaps a stronger measure of community integration than socialization with familiar persons.

Before discussing generic activities, it should be noted that the majority of OMH (66 percent) and OMR (87 percent) residents did participate in activities held at or sponsored by the state facility. Participation in employment, even sheltered workshops, was low. The fact that participation in department programs was not universal is due both to the age of the residents and the lack of availability of appropriate programs or of transportation to such programs. One provider in the OMH system also commented on the lack of financial resources for the residents:

"There should be more community activities available for residents; the hospital should provide entertainment for residents they place in family care. The association for care providers should try to get cheaper rates for residents at the YMCA. Should provide recreation two or three times a week for the residents. Residents should have more money. If they can't have enough money to enjoy society, why should they bother to reintegrate themselves?"

The issue of community participation is becoming increasingly important as the life expectancy of mentally retarded persons increases. According to Stroud and Murphy (1984), if these persons are to retire from departmental work programs, they will need to increase their skills to participate in generic services, i.e., those services provided for all persons in the community, not just for those with special needs.

The level of participation in other community activities was infrequent. Table 4.6 shows the level of participation in selected community activities (adapted from the integration in the community scale of Moos and Lemke [1979]). The two items asked in the first study differed from those in the second and third studies, in which specific activities were individually addressed. It should be noted, however, that in the first study, group activities included those rehabilitation programs sponsored by the department, accounting at least partially for the difference between DSS and DMH residents. In addition, providers of care for the DSS residents remarked on the advanced age of this group, stating that age and infirmity kept them from greater participation. In general, participation in specific activities with the provider ranged from 6 percent of OMH residents going to movies to 93 percent of OMR residents going to meeting places. Participation in specific activities without the provider ranged from 12 percent of OMH residents going to parties to 55 percent of OMH residents going to restaurants. If we were to use a cutoff of monthly participation, the level of participation, of course, drops even further.

A couple of providers showed their own fears about the participation of their residents:

"They never participate in outside activities on a regular basis. They'd
much rather be happy right here. I wouldn't encourage that [out-
side activities], they might get hurt and I'm responsible."

"The residents just sit. They don't get into activities. Residents can't
go to town by themselves; they don't watch for cars when they

Table 4.6
Community Activities (%)

	DSS	DMH	OMH[a]	OMR[a]
(N)	(50)	(50)	(97–101)	(146–151)
Restaurant				
With provider	—	—	78	91
Without provider	—	—	55	34
Religious services				
With provider	—	—	29	54
Without provider	—	—	41	39
Parties				
With provider	—	—	27	76
Without provider	—	—	12	37
Meeting places				
With provider	—	—	21	93
Without provider	—	—	38	35
Clubs				
With provider	—	—	8	19
Without provider	—	—	14	17
Movies				
With provider	—	—	6	36
Without provider	—	—	21	27
Activities mean sum score				
With provider	(72)[b]	(84)[b]	(28.3)	(61.5)
Without provider	(11)[c]	(56)[c]	(30.3)	(31.5)

[a]Participation ranged from once a day to several times a year; once a year or less was considered nonparticipation.

[b]Residents participated with the family in activities outside the house at least once a month.

[c]Residents participated in outside activities, e.g., senior citizens centers, crafts groups, etc.,
at least monthly. N's were 131 and 99, respectively.

cross the street. The most capable resident is leaving tomorrow; he used to take them to town. I don't feel I should take them, as that would make them feel like kids."

Table 4.6 shows a striking contrast between the OMH and the OMR homes. The OMH residents participate in some activities more frequently without the provider than with, whereas the OMR residents participate much more frequently with the provider. The overall activities mean score demonstrates this clearly. On the average, participation without the provider was about the same for OMH and OMR residents, and was similar to participation with the provider for OMH residents. Participation was much higher with the provider for OMR residents.

As with the socialization measures, the provider clearly made more of a difference for the OMR residents than for the OMH residents. It appears that OMH residents are expected to be more independent than are OMR residents. (We cannot strictly compare the second and third studies with the first study, since the two items in the first study were not worded identically. However, results appear to be more consistent with the OMR study than with the OMH study.)

Summary of Community Participation. We have measured community participation in terms of the use of community resources, frequency of socialization, and participation in community activities. The results present a mixed picture. In terms of using services such as a doctor, barber, and grocer, we can conclude that these residents were able to partake of the community's resources. Nearly three-quarters of the residents used each of these resources. In contrast, their socializing with friends, relatives, and neighbors was, in general, considerably lower, as was their participation in generic community activities. On the average, nearly one-third of the residents socialized with the various components of the network and participated in the various generic community activities. The notable exception was participation by the OMR residents with their providers, where the average level of participation was elevated to 60 percent. We need to keep in mind that the criterion of participation was "at least several times a year," and that if the criterion is "at least monthly," participation drops even further.[1] Intercorrelation of the various measures to be presented in the next section will tell us whether it was the same persons who participated with and without the provider, or whether those who did not participate alone participated with the provider.

We do not have evidence to conclude that the residents are *active* members in the community. To some extent, their life in the community appears to be marginal rather than integral. Their use of resources, which has been described as a passive consumptive role (Segal and Aviram 1978), was much higher than their participation in activities or socialization. Perhaps most important, our studies have distinguished between participation with and without the provider. This distinction suggests the following:

• The care provider can have an important role as a facilitator of community integration.
• It is important to understand the nature of the provider's own participation in community life and how this relates to the resident.
• Program managers need to think carefully about the relative merits of participation with and without the care provider.
• It is important to address the issue of inappropriate dependency upon the provider.
• There is a need to assess each client with a view toward determining the proper match between the client and the provider.

These issues will be addressed more fully in the next chapter, which discusses the role of each actor in the foster care arrangement: the client, provider, and agency worker. We turn now to the prediction of community integration.

PREDICTION OF COMMUNITY INTEGRATION

Given that one goal of those departments placing residents in foster family care is integration into the community, what characteristics of the resident (e.g., age or ability), the provider (e.g., age or years

1. The use of resources question required simply a "yes" or "no" response.

in the community), and of the foster care homes (e.g., number of residents or household composition) might enhance or detract from such integration? If there are qualities that consistently lead to success, it would be useful to select clients, providers, or homes with such qualities.

The suggestions in the literature are far from clear-cut and usually do not focus on family care or the elderly. For example, Hull and Thompson (1981a, 1981b) found that the social structure of the facility and of the community were most predictive of the normalization of mentally retarded and mentally ill persons. Segal, Baumohl, and Moyles (1980) reported that types of neighborhoods predicted the community reaction to the mentally ill. Intagliata, Willer, and Wicks (1981) found that younger age and nonrural location were predictive of community involvement by persons who were mentally retarded, but that provider characteristics in general played a more crucial role in the adjustment of family care residents than did resident or community variables. Stroud and Murphy (1984) reported that social competence, verbal communication, and cognitive skills were associated with participation. Finally, in a study of VA homes in which foster care residents showed better social adjustment after four months than did those who remained in the hospital (with random assignment), Linn, Klett, and Caffey (1980) found that the number of clients in the home and the number of occupants were negatively associated with improvement in social functioning, while having children in the home was positively associated with improvement.

This section of the chapter examines those qualities that can predict community integration. Our first study focused on family integration; it was not until the second study that we focused on community integration. Thus, most of the analyses in this section begin with the second study and are replicated (with some modifications) in the third. Before turning to the major question of determining what qualities are related to community integration, we review both the outcome measures, i.e., the several measures of community integration used in our study, and the predictor measures, i.e., the several resident, provider, and home characteristics used in our analyses.

Outcome Measures

This chapter has presented the various measures of the extent to which the residents of adult foster family care met the objective of integration into the community. We observed that with minor exceptions they were passively *accepted* into the community, and encountered very little hostility or resistance. We then described several levels of *participation* and noted that most residents used generic community resources. In terms of their participation in informal social networks or more structured or formal community activities, participation was much less, with only about one-third taking part. Our data indicated substantial elevation of participation levels for OMR residents when they were accompanied by the care provider.

Our predictions thus used six different sum scores measuring the desired outcome of community integration. Mean sum scores were entered in the last row(s) of tables 4.3, 4.4, 4.5, and 4.6, and include one indicator of community acceptance—neighbor acceptance—and five indicators of community participation—use of community resources, socialization both with and without the provider, and activities both with and without the provider.[2]

In the first part of the results section we shall examine to what extent community acceptance (the first outcome measure) predicts community participation (the other outcome measures). Here we will briefly summarize the relationships among the indicators of community participation. First, we found that the use of resources was moderately related to the other four measures of participation. (The only exception was that use of resources was not related to socialization or activities with the provider in the OMH study, per-

2. It should be noted in table 4.3 that in the OMH study the neighbor acceptance sum score included five items and was from the resident responses, whereas in the OMR study the score included six items—with and without the provider were both included—and was based on providers' responses. It should also be noted that in table 4.6 the activity sum scores for OMR included only six activities, to be comparable with OMH. However, when sum scores were computed for prediction purposes, a seventh activity was included—plays/concerts—because the frequency was as high as some of the other activities in the OMR study. The average sum scores for six activities were very close to those for seven activities.

haps indicating again that the OMH residents arc expected to be more independent). With regard to the other four measures, we found that socialization with the provider present was related to activities with the provider. We also found that socialization without the provider was related to activities without the provider. This means that those who participate in social network interactions when the provider is present also will tend to participate in community activities with the provider. Likewise, those who participate in social network interactions when the provider is not present will tend to participate in community activities without the provider.

Somewhat surprisingly, activities with the provider present were *not* related to activities without the provider. This means that someone who participates in many community activities when the provider is present may participate in many or in very few when the provider is not present. Similarly surprising was the fact that socialization with the provider was not related to socialization without the provider in the OMH study, though it was related in the OMR study.

For the most part, then, the important distinction is not between the types of participation, but whether the provider is present or not. Participation comprises two clusters, participation with the provider present and participation without the provider, rather than distinct clusters of the use of resources, socialization, and activities. We shall need to keep this in mind when we look for predictors of community integration. That is, it is perhaps better to think of predicting participation with the provider present, and predicting participation without the provider, than of predicting participation in network socialization and predicting participation in community activities. We shall, however, keep the types of participation separate, in case different patterns of prediction are found, since, in any case, the types (socialization and activities) are not completely correlated.

Predictors

The predictors included characteristics of the resident, of the care provider, and of the home.

Resident characteristics:
• independent living abilities[3]
• length of stay in the family care home
• age
• proximity of relatives
• sex
• length of time institutionalized (OMH only)
• whether neighbors perceive resident as former patient (OMH only)
• how much resident perceives self having in common with neighbors (OMH only)
• marital status (OMH only)
• diagnosis (OMH only)
• psychological functioning (OMH only)
• expressive language ability (OMR only)
• receptive language ability (OMR only)
• intellectual level (OMR only)
• whether resident is Personal Care client[4] (OMR only)
• relatives' participation in activities with resident (OMR only)
• type of OMR day program engaged in
• other program participation (OMR only)

Provider characteristics:
• socialization sum score (described below)
• activities sum score (described below)
• age
• education
• length of time at address (OMR only)
• length of time in program (OMR only)
• marital status (OMR only)

3. Independent living abilities in study 2 were defined by a sum score measuring how the resident performed, independently or with reminders, fourteen tasks of everyday living that ranged from following a schedule and taking care of his or her personal appearance to handling spending money and using the telephone. Independent living abilities in study 3 were defined by a sum score measuring skills in the four tasks of cooking, shopping, using the telephone, and doing laundry.

4. The Personal Care program was developed for those clients with greater needs resulting from their greater functional and physical impairment. "Personal Care provided training for the providers, individualized services for each client, monitoring of service delivery, and increased reimbursement for services rendered" (State of New York, Office of Mental Retardation and Developmental Disabilities 1980:156).

Home characteristics:
- number of residents
- convenient access to services[5]
- rural or nonrural location
- age integration[6]
- access to public transportation
- household composition
- sex segregation (i.e., whether family care residents are same gender)
- close relationships among residents (see chapter 3) (OMH only)
- close relationships between provider and residents (see chapter 3) (OMH only)
- ethnic congruence between provider and residents (OMH only)
- ethnic congruence between provider and neighbors (OMH only)
- religious congruence between provider and residents (OHM only)
- presence of Personal Care clients in home (OMR only)
- type of housing in neighborhood (i.e., multiple- or single-family units or farmhouses) (OMR only)

Provider Socialization and Activities. As the care provider in family care is charged with facilitating the community integration of the residents, it is essential to understand the nature of his or her own participation in community life. Not only does this information tell us what perhaps more typical community residents are doing; it also gives us a threshold for expectation from the residents. That is, it is unlikely that a typical foster resident would participate more actively than his or her foster care provider. Further, on an individual basis, we are able to examine the relationship between the provider's level of participation and that of his or her residents. The provider can help to pave the way for the resident to enter the new setting.

Participation of the providers, at least several times a year, was quite widespread, and roughly comparable for OMH and OMR pro-

5. Convenient access to services, adapted from Segal and Aviram's (1978) community accessibility scale, measured accessibility to ten facilities, including such places as shops, a park, a library, and a barbershop.
6. Age integration was defined as an age difference between the youngest and the oldest family care resident of 15 years or more.

viders, in informal networks (90 percent) and in going to restaurants (95 percent) and religious services (84 percent). Participation was lower for OMH than OMR providers in going to parties (68 percent and 85 percent, respectively), meeting places (59 percent and 91 percent), and movies (22 percent and 45 percent). In general, providers may go to clubs (40 percent, both OMH and OMR) and movies less frequently because of unavailability, expense, or the necessity of advance planning and obtaining respite support for their residents. Combining across friends, relatives, and neighbors, the *socialization mean score* was 91.0 for OMH providers and 90.1 for OMR providers. Combining across the six activities of restaurants, religious services, parties, meeting places, clubs, and movies, the *activities mean score* was 61.1 for OMH providers and 73.3 for OMR providers. What is more noteworthy for our purposes is that participation, overall, was so much higher for providers than for residents in both the OMH and OMR homes. However, when OMR residents were accompanied by the provider, the participation levels in some of the activities were comparable.

Having reviewed both the outcome measures of community integration and the measures used to predict community integration, we turn now to the results of our analyses.

Community Acceptance as a Predictor of Community Participation. Our first analysis addressed the question of the extent to which community acceptance is a necessary prerequisite for community participation. We found that in OMH homes neighbor acceptance was related to activities without the provider ($r = .17$, $p < .05$), but not to use of resources, nor to activities with the provider. In OMR homes neighbor acceptance was related to use of resources ($r = .19$, $p < .05$), activities with the provider ($r = .22$, $p < .01$), and activities without the provider ($r = .17$, $p < .05$). Since correlations cannot establish causality, it is possible that there is a reciprocal interaction between acceptance and participation. Beyond a minimal baseline of acceptance, increased participation may foster increased familiarity with and acceptance of these residents in the community. In other words, since the residents do not appear to have qualities that would be threatening to other community members, perhaps increased contact leads to a positive attitude change.

While four of the correlations are statistically significant, it is clear that community acceptance does not account for a large proportion of the variance in community participation. We turn now to the other variables that might predict both acceptance and participation.

Resident, Care Provider, and Home Characteristics as Predictors of Community Integration

In the second and third studies, two types of analyses were conducted; first a set of predictors was related to the outcome variables in bivariate analyses. Then based on the results of the bivariate analyses, a subset of predictors was entered into a multiple regression analysis. Tables 4.7, 4.8, and 4.9 show all variables related to any one measure of community integration (at $p \leq .05$). The tables present statistically significant results for the bivariate analyses. Results from regression analyses will be presented when they contribute beyond the bivariate results.

Resident Characteristics. Keeping in mind the distinction between with and without the provider, in general, resident characteristics were most useful in predicting activities without the provider, use of resources, and to some extent socialization without the provider (see table 4.7). Independent living abilities and expressive language were, for the most part, positively associated with community integration. The regression analyses also provided further support for the length of stay in the home and age as predictors. Living in the home for a longer time appears to provide the resident with acceptance by neighbors and the confidence to venture into the community. On the other hand, the older the resident, the less we find independent participation or use of resources. As might be expected, the longer the OMH resident had been institutionalized, the less he or she was independently involved with the community.

Provider Characteristics. As shown in table 4.8 provider characteristics are clearly more useful in predicting participation with the provider than participation without. Also, provider characteristics appear to be more important for OMR residents than for OMH

Table 4.7

Resident Characteristics as Predictors of Community Integration: Bivariate Relationships

| | Neighbor Acceptance | | Use of Resources | | With Provider | | | | Without Provider | | | |
| | | | | | Socialization | | Activities | | Socialization | | Activities | |
	OMH	OMR	OMH	OMR	OMH	OMR	OMH	OMR	OMH	OMR	OMH	OMR
Independent living abilities			.27[c]	.18[a]			-.33[d]		.30[c]	.15[a]	.33[d]	.28[d]
Length of stay in home		.15[a]				.17[a]						.22[c]
Age				-.18[a]					-.31[c]		-.27[c]	-.21[c]
Proximity of relatives	.18[a]							-.16[a]			.28[c]	
OMH Only:												
Length of time institutionalized			-.22[a]						-.31[d]		-.23[a]	
Neighbors perceive resident as former patient							.24[a]					
Qualities perceived in common with neighbors			-.37[d]						-.29[c]		-.21[a]	
OMR Only:												
Expressive language				.16[a]		.17[b]				.20[c]		.23[c]
Receptive language				.23[c]		.15[a]						.24[c]
Intellectual level												.15[a]
Whether resident is												
Personal Care client				(2.13)[e]								
Relatives' participation in activities with resident				(2.31)[e]								
Type of day program				(2.46)[f]								

Note: Except as indicated below, all values are Pearson product-moment correlations.

[a]$p \leq .05$

[b]$p \leq .01$

[c]$p \leq .005$

[d]$p \leq .001$

[e]t-value; $p < .05$

[f]F-value; $p < .05$. Those in workshop or employment situations have highest levels of usage, and those attending senior centers the lowest.

Table 4.8

Provider Characteristics as Predictors of Community Integration: Bivariate Relationships

| | Neighbor Acceptance | | Use of Resources | | With Provider | | | | Without Provider | | | |
| | | | | | Socialization | | Activities | | Socialization | | Activities | |
	OMH	OMR	OMH	OMR	OMH	OMR	OMH	OMR	OMH	OMR	OMH	OMR
Provider's socialization		.37[d]		.14[a]		.36[d]	.20[a]	.25[d]				
Provider's community activities	.21[a]	.34[d]		.28[d]	.19[a]	.25[d]	.30[c]	.69[d]			.25[b]	
Provider's education				.20[b]		.23[c]		.32[d]				
Age				−.21[b]								
OMR Only:												
Length of time at address		.28[d]				.14[a]						
Length of time in program								−.25[d]				.13[a]

Note: All values are Pearson product-moment correlations.

[a] p ≤ .05
[b] p ≤ .01
[c] p ≤ .005
[d] p ≤ .001

residents. Provider characteristics are also of some use for OMR residents in predicting use of resources and neighbor acceptance. In particular, the greater the provider's socialization and activities, the greater the resident's integration. Knowing this association should prove to be useful in selecting and training providers. Related to this, we find that OMR providers' education is related to residents' participation with the provider and use of resources; this might mean that the more highly educated providers are engaging in more activities and socialization, particularly since the provider's education is not related to independent participation by residents. We found, though, that in the OMR regression analysis, which included providers' activity and socialization level, providers' education was associated independently with resident activities with the provider. Perhaps this means that those providers who are more highly educated are more sensitive to the needs of their residents, or to training directed toward involving residents in activities.

Home Characteristics. As shown in table 4.9, home characteristics surprisingly do not predict use of resources or neighbor acceptance. They are also not very useful for predicting participation with the provider, especially for OMR residents. Home characteristics are most predictive of participation without the provider. The most useful home characteristics are the number of residents (negatively associated with supported participation for OMH residents; positively associated with independent participation for OMR residents) and access to services. The regression analyses indicate that a resident in an OMR home with Personal Care residents is more likely to use community resources, socialize without the provider, and have higher acceptance by neighbors.

Summary of Resident, Provider, and Home Characteristics as Predictors. It appears that the most useful characteristics, overall, for predicting community integration are independent living abilities, length of stay in the home, resident's age, provider participation, number of residents, and convenient access to services. The importance of carefully defining desired outcomes is clear from the above results. That is, if independent participation is the desired goal, departments doing placement should select on the basis of

Table 4.9

Home Characteristics as Predictors of Community Integration: Bivariate Relationships

	Neighbor Acceptance		Use of Resources		With Provider				Without Provider			
					Socialization		Activities		Socialization		Activities	
	OMH	OMR	OMH	OMR	OMH	OMR	OMH	OMR	OMH	OMR	OMH	OMR
Number of residents					-.36[d]		-.25[c]	-.25[b]		.16[a]		.16[a]
Convenient access to services									.32[d]		.43[d]	.27[d]
Rural location											(3.58)[e]	(4.32)[f]
Age integration					(3.16)[g]			(4.60)[h]				
Access to public transportation		(-1.99)[i]										
OMH Only:												
Close relations among residents									.20[a]			
Close relations between provider and resident											.18[a]	
OMR Only:												
Personal Care clients in home										(2.11)[i]		
Multiple- or single-family housing in neighborhood												(4.55)[e]

Note: Except as indicated below, all values are Pearson product-moment correlations.

[a] $p \le .05$
[b] $p \le .01$
[c] $p \le .005$
[d] $p \le .001$
[e] F-value; $p < .05$
[f] F-value; $p < .01$.
[g] F-value; $p < .05$. Single-client homes had highest participation.
[h] F-value; $p < .05$. Age-segregated homes had highest participation.
[i] t-value; $p < .05$.

resident and home characteristics. Alternatively, if supported participation (that is, community activity and socialization while accompanied by the care provider) is the desired result, agencies should make placements based on provider characteristics. Likewise, if the departments wish to enhance the use of community resources, they should select on the basis of resident characteristics, and additionally for OMR on the basis of provider characteristics. Finally, if the departments wish to enhance neighbor acceptance, provider characteristics are of some help. (It is difficult to predict neighbor acceptance at all for OMH—perhaps because the measure of outcome was the resident's perception.)

For the most part, patterns of prediction were the same for informal social network participation and for community participation, and the larger differences were between independent participation and supported participation. This is not surprising, given the pattern of intercorrelations presented earlier. In other words, in most respects we have participation with or without the provider, such participation including both informal social network interaction and community activities.

COMMUNITY INTEGRATION: A MIXED PICTURE

It is useful to think about deinstitutionalization into foster family care along a continuum of permeability. The first point along the continuum is represented by mere residence with the family. The next point is integration into the family. These points were described in the previous chapter. The next level includes moving outside the security of the family to use generic community resources (table 4.4). After that we find passive acceptance by neighbors and others in the community, as shown in tables 4.1 through 4.3. Further along the continuum we find deeper levels of penetration reflected in the socialization and community activity scores with and wiithout the care provider, as shown in tables 4.5 and 4.6. As we have indicated earlier, the life of the residents in the community appears to be marginal rather than integral. Their use of resources was higher than their integration with neighbors or their participation in socialization or activities.

Because of the relatively small size and familiarity of a family care home, we hypothesized that there would be little opposition to this setting. Our hypothesis was confirmed. Community acceptance was found to be high. For all three of our populations, warm and friendly reactions from neighbors and others in the community were reported, and almost no hostility was experienced. An element of superficiality to these relationships was noted, however. A sizable minority reported indifference to the family care home. Although most residents had met their neighbors, fewer had been invited into neighbors' homes or said they had real friends in the neighborhood. There was some indication that neighbor acceptance was enhanced by informal network relationships, as facilitated by the proximity of a resident's relatives, and the provider's participation in socialization and activities. Both relatives and care providers appear to assist or mediate in promoting community acceptance.

Moving from a superficial acceptance, or tolerance, we considered the extent to which residents are part of the community rather than merely residing in the community. Our study supports this distinction. If we compare, for example, the frequency of participation in psychiatric or developmental center activities with the frequency of participation in generic activities, the former are found to be much higher. In light of the high level of acceptance that was found, we noted that a concomitantly high level of resident participation in the community was not observed.

As noted earlier, one of the most significant aspects of our findings pertaining to socialization and community activities was the distinction between participation with and without the provider. It is important for program managers to consider the relative merits of independent and supported participation. Participation along with the care provider can facilitate integration into the community in two ways. For the resident it serves to extend the security of the home, through the relationship with the care provider, into the unfamiliar community environment. Such internal support systems that facilitate external integration have been described as being particularly important to older persons (David, Moos, and Kahn 1981; Segal and Aviram 1978). Second, for members of the community, it provides a familiar frame of reference through which they can meet the stranger. The resident has an identity and role as part of the resident/care provider relationship, rather than being part of an anonymous group of mentally disabled. The association of the resident with the familiar care provider can decrease the resistance to the inclusion of the mentally disabled person.

On the other hand, participation without the care provider signifies that some level of independence has been reached. While participation with the provider varied directly with the care provider's participation level, there was little association between the provider's participation and the resident's independent participation. Although the provider might serve as a role model for community participation, this effect apparently did not extend to participation without the provider. (It is important to note here that if we wish to encourage independent participation, consideration also must be given to the home's convenient access to services. The resident also should have enough money and financial skill to allow participation at the same level as other members of the community.)

Results of a study such as this dealing with deinstitutionalized or frail persons must be viewed not in absolute terms, but relative to realistic expectations regarding the population. First, we need to compare their level of community integration with that of the usual community residents. Some indication was provided by the provider's level of participation, which was in general found to be higher than residents'. Second, community integration must be understood in the context of the levels of integration afforded by other residential alternatives for the older mentally ill and mentally retarded. For this comparison, we turn to related literature.

In Segal and Aviram's (1978) study of residents of California's sheltered care facilities, low levels of participation similar to our findings were reported in community groups, community recreational facilities, educational activities, and activities such as going to a bar or on a date, using credit or a bank account, and working. Paradoxically, in the Horizon House Institute's (1975) assessment of the life adjustment of former mental patients, in which a low level of participation was also reported, although half the respondents stated that they wanted more social activity and involvement than they were experiencing, over three-quarters stated that overall they were satisfied with their social lives.

Segal and Aviram (1978) also caution that many of the persons they and we are studying had never been active participants in their communities; many had never married and many had spent a major part of their adult lives in institutions. They generally had had a low level of education and limited steady employment for longer than one year. Thus, unless a great deal of social training is provided, many avenues of social life and employment are closed to these groups.

The present results should also be compared with those obtained in a study by David, Moos, and Kahn (1981) of elderly residents of sheltered care settings. The authors found that elderly persons in both residential care and independent apartments had fairly low levels of community integration, and integration into the community was almost nonexistent for residents of skilled nursing facilities. However, Hochschild (1973), in a study of elderly persons in a senior citizens apartment complex, observed the value of integration within the facility as a valuable source of satisfaction and well-being despite the lack of external integration.

It is essential that each resident be encouraged to participate to the greatest degree comfortable while perhaps at the same time stretching his or her abilities and capabilities. Family care is able to promote such participation particularly through the involvement of the care provider and a reasonably high level of community acceptance. It is also, however, critical to assess realistically each client's potential for participation. Our data indicate that individual characteristics such as age and independence capacity give some indication as to whether a particular client can reasonably be expected to function independently of the care provider. Therefore, at the beginning of placement, treatment plans can reflect this expectation and be transmitted directly to the care provider. For those whose ability to function independently is limited, a particular strength of family care is its ability to provide meaningful interactions both with other residents in the foster family, and with the care provider and her family.

Perhaps expectations for community integration are excessive. It is now recognized that not all residents have the potential to move out of family care and live independently. By the same token, it may be necessary to rethink community integration. It is essential that program planners focus attention upon the appropriate and satisfactory level of interaction for their clients. Integration may best be understood not in global terms but rather in terms of focused goals based on the ability of each resident to participate. In the next chapter we turn to the role played by each actor in family care, and focus on the agency worker as transmitting goals for the client to the provider.

Summary: In this chapter we explored the extent to which the residents became a part of the larger community. Both neighbors and others in the community were friendly and warm to the family care residents. Almost no hostility was experienced. It was clear, however, that the absence of opposition did not necessarily constitute acceptance into the life of the community. Many reported a reaction of indifference. It might be more accurate to describe the situation of the residents as tolerated rather than accepted. Residents were found to use the resources of the community, e.g., the doctor, beauty shop/barber, grocery. In contrast, their socializing with friends, relatives, and neighbors was, in general, considerably lower, as was their participation in generic community activities. The notable exception was participation by the OMR residents in the company of their providers, where the average level of participation was nearly doubled. Provider characteristics were most useful in predicting supported participation, while resident and home characteristics were most useful in predicting independent participation.

5 · The Actors in Foster Family Care

Aptekar defined the foster home placement as a triangular frame-work in which the worker must be oriented to the needs and at-titudes of the client, the home, and the procedures of the agency. He described the agency worker as the important connecting link between the client and the family. "Rules and regulations are help-ful only when they are seen in relation to the psychology of the client; the worker's task, therefore, is a psychological and not just a procedural one" (1965:354). This chapter will examine the roles of the various actors as they interact in the creation of the foster family. In addition to the foster family, the client, and the case-worker, we will include the "natural" family of the resident, al-though it will be seen that their role is minimal. The care provider, client, and natural family will be described first, followed by the caseworker, whose role is to link the other actors in the system.

CARE PROVIDER

The importance of the care provider to family care success has been noted by Intagliata and Willer (1981). Of all the actors, perhaps the heaviest demands are placed on the host family, yet it is largely unknown how much the system can rely on an innate desire to create a "family." Are these foster families more or less able than are natural families to care for less well-functioning members? Titmuss (1968), for example, believed that community-based care was a step backward, since it transferred care from a trained staff (in the institutions) to untrained persons (i.e., the family) who also have less in the way of physical accommodations. On the other hand, one could see these characteristics as virtues rather than limitations. We might point, for example, to the informal nature of the provision of services and to rootedness in the community as significant assets.

A distinguishing feature of family care is the informal provision of services. The vast literature documenting the benefits of informal supports also recognizes the strains involved in providing informal support. The primary care giver in family care, as noted earlier, is not a professional nor even an employee within a mental health setting. Rather, the care giver is a member of the community given the responsibility of caring for clients within the natural setting of his or her own home. Ideally the care giver and the service setting resemble the situation of a family member caring for a frail or disabled older relative. In both cases immediate and direct care and the determination of the emotional tone of the setting are the responsibility of a nonprofessional. As Jacobson, Schwartz, and Janicki (1984) noted, for those clients in foster family settings, intensive intervention activities will typically be carried out in agency or clinic settings. Willer and Intagliata (1984) note, however, some trends toward increasing the professionalization of family care providers, as evidenced by specialized training, salary, and provider associations.

In saying that family care homes are rooted in the community, we mean that the residents are placed in a home which had existed in the community prior to being a residence for frail persons. The care provider and her family have an ongoing relationship and association with the community. By contrast, other residential alternatives for the frail are newly placed in the community, and relationships must be developed on that basis. Further, they are staffed by persons who are often as much newcomers and strangers as are the residents. This one feature alone suggests possible differences in the normalization offered by family care as contrasted to community residences.

Intagliata, Crosby, and Neider (1981) refer to the importance of the provider for residents' participation in community activities. A care provider who is active and visible in the community may pave the way for the inclusion of residents into community life. The care provider can increase community members' receptivity to the resident through their familiarity with the care provider and can serve as a role model for participation. In the next sections we describe some of the typical providers, both in the literature and in our studies, discuss providers' motivation and perceived rewards, and address the provider's role in promoting integration into the community. In this way, we weave together some of the strands described separately in earlier chapters.

Portraits of Providers

Even if there are more members in the provider family, generally there is one person with primary responsibility for the residents. In our studies we defined the person who was at home most of the time as the primary care provider. (In the literature this person is variously referred to as the caretaker, foster parent, manager, sponsor, operator).

Several authors have examined homes with different types of care givers. Good characteristics of foster home parents identified by Browder, Ellis and Neal (1974) were acceptance of the client's handicap and maintenance of good relationships with agencies. Collins and Pancoast (undated) drew a composite picture of the typical provider drawn from their contacts with fifty-two boarding homes. These boarding homes were similar to foster homes in that the providers were paid with public funds but were not employees of any hospital or the welfare department. Rather, they were "independent entrepreneurs who chose to care for this specialized population and did so with minimal supervision and no formal training" (p. 51). Collins and Pancoast described

a woman about 60 years of age with extensive previous work experience in caretaking occupations such as practical nursing, cooking or foster care.

She has been married [though she currently may be] widowed or divorced. Her stated reasons for becoming a home provider and specializing in the care of mentally handicapped persons are a combination of needing extra income, liking people and wanting to help people. . . . They feel that they are performing a real service in helping their residents adjust to the community and in meeting their needs for care. They live with the residents twenty-four hours a day and, except for shopping which is a major activity, seldom leave the home. (p. 51)

And on page 53:

While we did encounter two or three grossly substandard and unscrupulous home providers, we were generally impressed with the quality of care and the dedication of the home providers. The real nucleus of the home care system consisted of the women described above. With no formal training and little encouragement from agencies but with a great deal of understanding and experience in living, they have created an occupation. Significantly, many of these women are known to one another and in frequent communication by telephone. They recruit other suitable providers into the business, give each other advice about food, problems with their boarders and a host of other matters and "pass the word" about troublesome residents or agency personnel. Their boarders tend to have a lower hospitalization rate than those of home providers who do not take a personal interest in or spend time with their residents or see the home solely as a source of income rather than a satisfying vocation.

Vandivort, Kurren, and Braun (1984) report a somewhat different type of provider in a program for frail elderly persons in Hawaii. These providers were primarily in their 30s or 40s, with children at home and saw the client as serving a grandparent role for their children.

The official publication of the New York State Office of Mental Health, *This Month in Mental Health* (Wehmeyer 1981), described care providers typical of those in the system. One was a woman living with her husband and their six children in a large, two-story home in a medium-size city. She provided a home for four elderly women from one of the state psychiatric centers. "They're good women," the provider said. "They're clean and neat and they care about each other." She reported, "I was hesitant about getting involved for quite a while, but when I talked with some people who were participating, I found out that it wasn't really as difficult as I had thought so I decided to give it a try."

As reported more fully in chapter 2, the providers in our studies were predominantly middle-aged women. About 60 percent were married. Over one-half of the families included husband and wife and over one-quarter also included children. For the 20 percent or so who would otherwise have been living alone, it appeared that rather than the residents coming into a "traditional" family, the residents and the care provider actually helped to create a family for each other.

About half of the care providers in our studies were high school graduates, with about one-fifth having at least some college. These findings are consistent with those of Adams (1975), who reported that studies of foster care parents have consistently described a group from middle and lower socioeconomic strata, and with Epple (1982), who described the New York family care group as having predominantly a high school level of education.

In our studies the care provider had been in the program an average of about six years. According to Wehmeyer (1981), providers tend to remain with the program for many years once they become part of it. She cited a woman in one small town who had been a family care provider for thirty-two years; her mother had been one of the first providers in New York State. The providers in our studies tended to be long-term residents of their communities with about three-quarters having resided in the community for at least ten years.

The typical provider in our studies appeared loving and caring. We visited one home the day after Mother's Day, and the two elderly residents were still wearing the corsages which had been presented to them by their provider. Some typical provider comments were: "I like my life. I really like to make an older person happy. When they kiss you good night, what more can you ask?" "If I couldn't treat 'em right I'd close down my doors." "I love them and if anything happens to them it hurts me." "If you care for people as a family member, that feeling is really the most important thing to give to them." "I once sat up all night with a resident who was afraid of a thunderstorm."

Motivations and Rewards

In their report of a hospital-sponsored foster care program, Oktay and Volland (1981) reported that providers were motivated by humanitarian aims, strong religious convictions, and a wish to keep the elderly patients out of nursing homes. Although increased income was important, it was not a primary motivation. Mor, Sherwood, and Gutkin (1986) found that the primary motivation to become a provider in small residential care homes was to help people. Another important motivation was to have company. These patterns appear to be common, across a wide variety of studies, with a wide variety of clients and providers, and were found in our research as well.

This Month in Mental Health (Wehmeyer 1981) described a family care provider who commented on the motivations and rewards of the program. This man lives with his wife in a large home on the outskirts of a city. Their two children are grown and no longer live at home. Atypically, perhaps, this man is the family care provider while the wife works outside the home. He stays at home, cooks the meals, and tends the house. He is emphatic about why he became a family care provider. "Not for the money. If money is your motive, don't get involved in this program. We do the most work and get the least money. But we also get the most satisfaction."

Reporting on the Foster Family Care Pilot Project in Massachusetts, Dale (1980) listed as the reasons for care giver satisfaction: the opportunity to help others, the companionship, and the financial support. Aspects of the program the providers liked least were inadequacy of financial remuneration, lack of respite care and feeling of confinement, lack of privacy, and difficulties of dealing with incontinence and sleeplessness. Changes they would like made were having more background information on the participants, more participant involvement in activities outside the home, and more transportation available to the participants. These results were nearly identical to our findings.

In our first study care givers were asked, "What are some of the rewards of being a care giver?" Although 44 percent reported they initially had had financial reasons for joining the program, only 8 percent listed financial gain as one of the rewards. Personal satisfaction was offered by 70 percent of the respondents as a major reward of being a provider. Other important rewards were improvement of the resident (30 percent) and companionship (22 percent).

When the providers in our study were asked, "What are some of the disadvantages or drawbacks of being in the program?" only 14 percent listed not enough money. The chief drawback was being tied down, cited by nearly half the care givers. Over one-fourth said there were no disadvantages.

Several of the providers in our studies described how they first became involved in the program. Many had had previous experience in long-term care institutions. Some viewed family care as an opportunity to correct some of the flaws they had observed in other settings for the elderly:

- Mrs. A., 43 years old, has been with the program for eleven years. She had previously worked at some rest homes, where she "saw some crummy homes; for example, watered-down juice, residents begging the staff for food."

- Mrs. B. is 41 years old and a college graduate. Her husband is employed out of the home. Mrs. B. explained, "I used to work as a nurse in a nursing home and was appalled by the lack of personal attention and care those people were getting. I wanted to do something for them, but I knew there was really nothing I could do until I heard about this program. Now I get personal happiness out of doing something for others."

For others, the program fit into their other family needs, and they found it rewarding to provide service.

- Miss C. has lived in the community for over ten years, and has been with the program for five years. She has worked with people all her life and, in particular, with the elderly since she was 18. Previously she had worked in a nursing home and in a cafeteria. "My father was living with me. In order to stay home with my father I started my own rest home. I am just so happy that the Lord can give me the opportunity to take care of these people."

• Mrs. D. is 69 and married. She has been in the program for twenty years. When her daughter went away to college, "I had room and my neighbor told me about the program. If I had the chance I would do it all over again—I like the work."

• Mrs. E. is 60 years old and has lived in the community all her life. She had worked at a convalescent hospital, a doctor's office, and a hospital, and had been director of nursing at a nursing home. She became involved in the program because it was an opportunity to work at home, and because she needed the income, as her husband is on Social Security.

Still others entered the program because of the needs of a particular resident:

• Mrs. F., a 56-year-old widow, lives next to her daughter. Mrs. F.'s eight grandchildren were all present. Mrs. F. had lived in the community for over fifteen years, and is well known in the community. Mrs. F. stated that she had always liked taking care of people. "I took care of Mrs. X in her home. When she had her stroke, she needed more care. Someone suggested joining this program."

Finally, some of the providers were already caring for the client, and then learned that they needed to be licensed to do so.

• Mrs. G., a 67-year-old widow, was formerly a nurse's aide in a nursing home. She has lived in the community for over twenty years. "I had residents before and then a year ago the state came and said I had to get a license. These are the only residents I have had."

After describing typical providers and their motivations and rewards for being in the program, we next focus on the role of the provider as a bridge between the formal and informal support system. As we have said above, family care is an informal support system with a care provider who has roots in the community. This enables her to fulfill two important goals of the program: to connect the client to community resources and to introduce the client to other informal community supports, such as neighbors.

The Provider as Community Link

In addition to her function as primary care giver, the provider is also the link between the formal and informal support systems, thereby promoting the integration of residents into the community. Bjaanes and Butler (1974) found that the resident's independence was associated with participation by the care provider. Clearly, the creation of home environments that are conducive to family integration are, to a large extent, dependent on the care provider. Our data presented in the previous chapter, however, point to an additional role for the care provider, that of facilitator of community integration. Intagliata, Crosby, and Neider (1981) cite a number of studies indicating a positive relationship between family care residents' use of community activities and being accompanied by the care provider or other supervising adult.

Some of the literature points to the adverse outcomes that result when providers discourage community integration. For example, Bercovici (1981) found that residents of small group homes for mentally retarded persons were not only not shown how to go out into the community but were discouraged from using community resources or establishing relationships with other persons. Aanes and Moen (1976) noted that residents of group homes (using a foster family care model) did not show gains in expected self-direction. They reasoned that the more independent and persistent residents would be perceived as demanding more from the group home parents.

Intagliata, Willer, and Wicks (1981; see also Willer and Intagliata 1984) classified seventy-seven family care providers into two groups, according to caseworkers' assessments of their overall performance: high quality and low quality. High-quality home care givers encouraged clients' development of new skills and use of community resources. In terms of personal characteristics, high-quality care givers were better educated, had more health-related training, and were more likely to be motivated by previous experience with the mentally retarded (through a family member or employment).

According to departmental regulations, the providers are expected to integrate the client into the community. The Department of Social Services, for example, states that "the operator shall maintain a program of social support which shall include . . . providing opportunities to participate in individual or family activities within or outside of the home" (State of New York, Department of Social Services 1984:21). It is perhaps unreasonable to expect residents to participate more actively outside the home than do the providers. Therefore, care provider activities are important as a baseline against which to measure resident activities.

In our second and third studies we found that care providers participated more frequently in informal activities such as spending time with friends, relatives, or neighbors, going to parties, and eating in restaurants than in more formal activities. Attending religious services appeared to be a regular activity for a large number. Activities that require more advance planning, e.g., attending various events or clubs, were engaged in less frequently and, indeed, may have been largely unavailable or too costly. A somewhat higher level of attendance at plays, concerts, movies, parties, and meeting places was reported by OMR providers than by OMH providers, thus affording greater potential for resident participation.

In our second study OMH care providers were asked to describe the actions they took to encourage their residents to engage in community activities. Nearly all the care providers said they tried in some way to encourage participation, although 13 percent said it was not necessary since the resident participated on his or her own initiative. The most frequently cited methods for encouraging participation were taking the residents along when the care provider went shopping, to the movies, or to church, or transporting the residents to places where they could take part in psychiatric center activities, community resources, or visits. Nearly one-quarter introduced residents to friends and neighbors, and one-fifth gave verbal encouragement for participating. Wehmeyer (1981) found the residents she talked to enthusiastic about the providers' efforts: "Mrs. D. always has time for us . . . we go shopping and out to eat . . . we help each other get along." Another woman reported: "I feel as though this has been my home all my life. Here I am free; I don't feel like a patient. B. and P. treat me like an equal, as if we were related."

While recognizing the important role of the provider as a facilitator of community integration, we must, at the same time, note the issue of dependency which has been raised with regard to family care (Baker, Seltzer, and Seltzer 1974). It is necessary to sort out whether this is inappropriate dependency or appropriate facilitation by the care provider. Our data suggest that residents in OMR homes but not in OMH homes are dependent on their providers for much of their participation in activities. Since participation without the provider is roughly comparable between the two populations, this would suggest that rather than a reflection of inappropriate dependency on the provider in OMR homes, the difference in participation with the provider represents appropriate facilitation by the provider—participation that should be encouraged.

Since fewer than half the residents participated in activities without the care provider, and since for residents in the OMR study the level was elevated when they participated with the provider, we have demonstrated not only the importance of finding appropriate providers, but the need to assess each client with a view toward determining the proper *match* between the client and the provider. In Kahana's theory of person/environment congruence (1982), if the person's needs and the environment's capacity to satisfy those needs are dissonant, the individual can change the environment, leave the field, or experience stress and discomfort. Since the residents of family care are less able to modify the environment or leave the field, the agency must carefully match the prospective family care resident with the provider. If the initial determination is that the resident will not be able to function totally or even partially independently and will need to rely heavily on the provider, a provider can be selected who not only urges the resident to participate in community activities, but who is an active participant herself and who can be encouraged to include the resident in her activities. In our third study we found that the provider's level of education was correlated with three measures of integration into the community: socialization and participation with the provider, and the use of community resources. This also has implications for selection, which we shall discuss later in this chapter.

In general, we have recommended that in both recruitment and training, care providers be sought who participate actively in the community and who through training can be encouraged to include residents in their activities. This is an important arena for inter-action between provider and resident. We turn now to focus on another participant in this interactive system, the client. In de-scribing the client's history, i.e., chronicity and length of stay in family care, it will be possible to examine whether clients are being selected whose needs are congruent with the demands of the family care environment.

CLIENT

Obviously there is a great deal of diversity in adult clients in foster family care. Among the clients we studied, the ages ranged from 18 to over 90. They ranged from the frail elderly to those with mental illness, to those with mental retardation/developmental dis-abilities. Of course, in any one home the diversity would be much smaller. Nevertheless, the overall theme descriptive of all the clients is that they are, by and large, a dependent population. It is im-portant, however, to perceive them in the foster family system, as in traditional families, as having reciprocal roles.

Seltzer, Seltzer, and Sherwood (1982) reported in a study of men-tally retarded adults that both the highest functioning and lowest functioning clients remained in the institution. The highest func-tioning clients considered the institution their home and did not want to move when offered a community placement. The lowest functioning were unable to make the transition. According to pro-gram managers in our study, most of the elderly residents of foster family care (from 60 to 95 percent, depending on the agency) had come from institutions. The residents in our studies had been in family care for various amounts of time. Some were new to the program. However, many had been in family care for a number of years. Across the three studies, 17 percent had been in family care for less than one year, while 36 percent had been in the program for over five years. Ten percent of the OMH residents and 13 per-cent of the OMR residents had been in the same home for over ten years. Five residents from OMH and five from OMR had been in the particular home for over twenty years. In our second study providers were asked how long they anticipated the residents would remain in the home. Ninety-five percent saw the stay as long-term or permanent.

For most of the older residents of all three programs, as discussed in an earlier chapter, it appears that adult foster family care is not usually a way station toward greater independence but, rather, the last stop before a skilled nursing facility or death. Foster care may shorten hospital stays and keep people out of nursing homes for a time. It may also help to prevent or delay reinstitutionalization.

The long-term residents in the family care home are thought of as family members. For example, Ms. S., aged 55, an OMR resident, had lived with the provider, Mrs. T., for twenty-six years (as long as Mrs. T. had been with the program). Ms. S. and three other residents were Personal Care clients. The eight women in the home were aged mid-30s to 64. Mrs. T. was 78, a widow, and lived with no other family. Ms. D., a former resident, had been in the family care home for sixteen years. She was the "family grandmother." The interviewer commented, "I saw a real family feeling." Foster family care is home for these people, and the roles and relationships in which they engage there are the focus of their lives. Thus, a good match between person and environment is critical for well-being.

Clients recently placed in family care include two groups: those coming from institutions and those coming from the community. Many of the clients placed in family care have previously been institutionalized for years, and have adapted to this life-style. For example, Ms. V., aged 75, was in the hospital for forty years before placement in Mrs. P.'s home. She has only been in family care for five months. Mrs. P. commented: "None of these residents have been in the house for more than six months [when Mrs. P. opened her family care home], and they consider each other as friends. Later they may feel more like family."

The group who have recently entered family care from the community present such problems as dealing with the loss of independence symbolized by placement, as well as perhaps a perceived loss of family members who heretofore were providing some support. As explained in an earlier chapter, a subgroup of these residents may have been hospitalized only long enough to stabilize their medications before placement into family care. This last group might be under some stress from having had to make two transitions in a short time, but presumably would not have lost their "community" skills.

Wehmeyer notes that OMH patients selected for family care are "chosen on the basis of their ability to care for themselves, as well as their ability to get along with other people" (1981:3). Adequate medical and psychological screening is essential before placement in foster family care no matter what the auspices, and whether the resident comes from an institution or from the community. In our studies it appeared that in the few instances of problems with neighbors and other members of the community, most of the problems could have been prevented with more adequate screening. Perhaps more training of the resident before entering the family and the community also could have precluded such incidents.

As we reported in chapter 3, when providers in our study were asked how they viewed the residents, over 85 percent reported viewing them as "family." Nevertheless, frequently the relationship is less like "normal" families with the elderly residents in the role of grandparents, and more like that of foster families for children. One provider, for example, remarked, "They're like little children. It's hard for them to be told what to do. Sometimes I have to scold them or send them to their room." Another comment that we deemed to be infantilizing was the following: "I don't allow them to watch the soap operas, only game shows and news. If they watch a soap opera and someone has an operation, they think they need one, too."

In our third study over 90 percent of the providers reported that their residents view their relationship with others in the house as family (this could refer to the provider's family or other foster residents), whereas in the first study only about 60 percent reported that the residents viewed each other as family. (It is possible that the discrepancy between the two studies might have arisen from the different question wordings.) At times the providers pointed out that the residents were not capable of sustaining friendships even within the household. These comments ranged from "One resident is slightly retarded and can't form friendships" to "The residents keep to themselves for the most part—do things in their own rooms—pray a lot." Providers also mentioned the self-consciousness of the residents as a reason for the residents' eating alone, rather than with the family or other residents. Preference for eating alone could be caused by embarrassment from noisy dentures, poor teeth, or blindness—or simply by long-standing patterns of solitary behavior as a result of living alone for many years.

While foster family care historically has been used primarily for the mentally ill and the mentally retarded, it is our contention that it could and should be used much more extensively by the frail elderly. Sainer et al. contend:

Most of these frail elderly have difficulty dealing with the complexity of the health and social service systems and many are hesitant and fearful to venture out of the familiarity of their neighborhoods. They are often adamant in their desire to maintain their independence and live in their own communities. Isolated and neglected they often fail to seek help until the point of crisis.

It has long been evident . . . that traditional approaches have not been too successful in reaching and serving this at-risk vulnerable group and that non-institutionalized community-based programs, especially focused on the frail elderly, are essential in order to provide the services needed to enable the elderly to maintain their independence as long as possible. (1977:1)

One of the reasons why foster care seems to be a good option is that the clients in question have no family supports to depend upon. Additionally, as one provider claimed, "Many times a resident can't get along with family but can get along much better with strangers. Children sometimes are unwilling to give up their social life to stay with elderly relatives." In the next section we examine the sorts of relationships the residents in our studies have with their "natural families."

THE "NATURAL FAMILY"

Little has been reported about the natural family of older residents in foster family care. Frail elderly persons who go into family care do so generally because they have no natural family who can take care of them, or the family they have is unwilling or unable to. In Markson's (1985) study of homes for the elderly and for the mentally ill, she found that very few of the residents had contact with relatives. In fact, many did not even know where their relatives were. Markson was able to visit some of the relatives and found that relatives of the retarded were more informative than relatives of the elderly and mentally ill.

Betts, Moore, and Reynolds (1981) refer to the "myth" that deinstitutionalized patients are better off living with their own families in their home communities. They claim that the families are frequently unprepared, ambivalent, or unwilling. Even for those who are willing, the care of mentally ill relatives can be stressful. In fact, it is frequently the adverse attitudes of family members toward deinstitutionalized relatives that contributes to chronic disability. As for clients in the OMR system, many were institutionalized precisely because their relatives were unable to provide for them. Also, as clients have aged, their relatives may have died. Parents or siblings may be frail themselves. For example, Mr. F., a 59-year-old man in our OMR sample, has a 90-year-old mother somewhere in New York State, but the provider does not know where. Mr. F. never sees or hears from her. Mr. R., aged 47, has an aunt living less than an hour away, but she is over 80, and "too old to come and visit or help out." In other words, we are witnessing the aging of the natural family helpers.

At the time of our study only about 5 percent of residents in DSS and MH homes were married, so most would not have a spouse as care giver. About one-fifth of the residents in the DSS homes and over one-half in the MH homes had never married, and would, therefore, be unlikely to have children to take care of them. Some of the residents, of course, have other extended family, such as siblings or nieces or nephews as part of their network.

In the second study we learned that a quarter of the residents had relatives living within a half hour of the foster homes, and only about one-third did not have any relatives within a two-hour ride. Nearly half the OMH residents were reported to spend time visiting with relatives at least several times a year. Most of these visits were without the care provider. By contrast, in the OMR homes almost two-thirds of the residents had no relative living within two hours of their homes. (Of those who had relatives living nearby, the relative was most frequently a sibling.) Not surprisingly, in the OMR homes only about one-quarter of the residents were reported to spend time visiting with relatives at least several times a year. In contrast to the OMH sample, half of those visiting with relatives visited both with and without the provider, and another 6 percent visited with relatives only in the presence of the provider. Only 7 percent visited only without the provider—as contrasted to 38 percent in the OMH sample, again reminding us of differences in the resident populations.

Much of the interaction involved the relative coming to visit and possibly taking the resident out to eat or to go shopping, or on other short trips. In the OMH study we found that the closer the resident lived to relatives, the higher was his or her level of participation in socializing and in activities in the community. In other cases the resident went to the relative's home—thereby providing some respite for the provider. In a few cases the interaction was only phone calls or sending gifts or letters.

In the first study nearly half the providers indicated that they were satisfied with the amount of participation of residents' relatives. However, an almost equal proportion reported they would like more contact with families of residents, and 6 percent said they wanted less involvement with relatives.

Some of the comments expressing satisfaction with the amount of contact included the following:

"Mr. Y.'s daughter came yesterday and had lunch with him; she comes practically every day. I like the relatives to visit because it makes the residents happy."

"The family comes and almost always takes them home for Thanksgiving and Christmas. The family is gracious and involved, but I don't want them underfoot all the time."

"When a family gives up their mother or father, they should let the care giver take over."

One of the providers explained how she enables residents to have contact with relatives:

"Residents talk on the phone and use the phone whenever they want. Even long distance. They pay me when the bill comes in. No one overdoes it."

Providers who wanted more contact with relatives commented:

"I would like to see the residents' family care more about them; it would help the residents tremendously."

"Mrs. X.'s stepson doesn't visit or call. I called him, but he won't come or call or even send a card."

Those providers who wished for less contact with relatives explained their reasons:

"I would like less involvement with the residents' families because you try to do your best and then the family tries to do something different."

In remarking that sometimes relatives don't understand older people, one provider explained that one resident's daughter complains that her mother doesn't wear a dress all the time, but the mother simply doesn't want to. "I can't force her to," she said, "she's not a child."

Another provider commented, "Sometimes it gets residents all nerved up when they see their relatives."

Finally, some providers expressed ambivalence, citing both the advantages and the strains:

Mrs. A. (82-year-old widow) is the provider for Mrs. B. (69-year-old widow). They have been together for three years. Mrs. B. goes to her relatives on holidays. She sees some of her relatives once a year, and goes to her brother or sister on weekends. She keeps bringing trinkets from home on weekends. Mrs. A. appreciates the relatives' taking Mrs. B. every weekend, but complained that Mrs. B.'s daughter was interfering in a dispute between Mrs. A. and Mrs. B. regarding Mrs. B.'s reading in bed at night. "The care provider should be boss of the house."

"I would like more involvement with the residents' families, but sometimes it's more damaging than good. Instead of a good visit, it can be a downer. Only if visitors don't lay their problems on the residents."

No matter for which system they provided homes for clients, most care providers reported only minimal interaction between residents and their families. In some cases attention by relatives was seen as dysfunctional.

THE AGENCY AS COORDINATOR

The last group of actors in the foster family care system includes the agency staff. For all three of the populations in our studies the formal organization of the foster care program begins at the state level, where rules and regulations are drafted and the overall operation is administered. Many states are currently facing the dilemma of either regulating the setting for safety with considerable monitoring of the degree of frailty permitted for residents of licensed facilities, or leaving the setting largely unregulated. If the former is done, "we are in danger of reinventing the restrictiveness of the nursing home. If the latter, there is the fear that a de facto unregulated neo-nursing home industry will spring up that is full of unknown abuses" (anonymous reviewer 1987).

In New York State, Family Care Advisory committees, composed of staff and providers, "meet quarterly at each facility to resolve issues including quality of care, timely receipt of provider payments, fire safety concerns, medication issues, training, and interpretation of policies and procedures" (State of New York, OMH 1983:42). The committee at each sponsoring agency makes suggestions to increase the program's effectiveness, recommends resolutions for provider-specific concerns, and comments on proposed procedures (State of New York, OMR 1986: 10.8.2, p. 1).

In the New York State Department of Social Services it is the responsibility of the county social service department to select homes that meet the requirements of the state regulations and to place the residents and supervise them. In the other two departments in

New York, the Office of Mental Health and the Office of Mental Retardation and Developmental Disabilities, supervisory responsibilities are covered by personnel within the state institutions or in the regional, district, or county office. There are generally Family Care case managers, who report to a Family Care coordinator.

Our framework of recruitment, matching of clients and homes, preplacement visits, training, and follow-up (Sherman and Newman 1979), is similar to the four-part framework Vandivort, Kurren, and Braun (1984) suggest is necessary for quality foster care: foster family recruitment and selection; training; client selection and matching; case management of foster placements. We focus here on the role that the agency worker plays in bringing together the other actors in the system. Using Vandivort, Kurren, and Braun's framework, it will be seen that in the first two stages the agency's interaction is with the provider; in the third stage the client is brought into the system; and finally, in the fourth stage the focus is on the continued interaction among provider, client, and agency staff. It should be emphasized that all of these functions serve to enhance the congruence of the foster care resident and the environment of the home.

Recruitment and Selection of Providers

Regardless of the system, one important role for the agency worker is in the area of recruitment of care providers. Most of the recruitment appears to be by word of mouth, although some media campaigns (newspapers, radio, and television) have been attempted (Brockett 1984; Collins and Pancoast undated; Talmadge and Murphy 1983; Vandivort, Kurren, and Braun 1984). Other places of recruitment include local churches, offices for the aging, and Parent Teacher Association meetings (Talmadge and Murphy 1983). Specifically, in New York State, recruitment is primarily by television and radio public service announcements, newspaper advertisements, transit cards on subways and buses, and word of mouth. Recently the New York State Office of Mental Health has initiated a recruitment campaign which additionally includes booklets in regional editions, a slide and tape presentation, and a Spanish-oriented booklet (State of New York, OMH 1986).

Typically, the most effective recruitment technique is through other providers. In our first study we found that many of the homes were self-selected through the acquaintance of either a friend or relative who had been a provider. There was more evidence of the providers' nominating themselves than of the caseworkers' locating them. According to agency management, it is not more difficult to recruit homes for geriatric residents than for other adults. (In fact, some providers prefer geriatric residents because the residents are seen as more passive.) A problem arises if the prospective residents have physical disabilities which would require more personal care and more supervision by the provider.

Prospective providers are screened by the clinical staff of the sponsoring agency. One family care coordinator at a state psychiatric center pointed out that selecting suitable family care providers is a painstaking process which generally takes several months and that those who are interested only in the financial aspects of the program are screened out at the initial contact. "While the provider certainly may be seeking supplemental income, he or she must be motivated in terms of getting personal satisfaction out of helping people. . . . We look for someone willing to commit himself or herself to this responsibility." A typical provider agreed: "Everyone who starts a place should be investigated before they start. A lot of them [care givers] do it just to get rich." It is interesting that the same question was raised in the last century over the controversial notion of paying foster parents who took in children. It was thought that acceptance of payment signified that the parents could not really care about the children (Zelizer 1985).

A Family Care coordinator commented that selecting providers is an intuitive process. She looks for "someone who is warm and caring, someone who is genuinely interested in other people; a person who gives me the feeling that he or she will do a good job." This attitude was reflected in the comment of the provider who told our interviewer, "You have to like to do it. You have to give a little love and care."

In a workshop sponsored by the National Institute of Mental Health (Carling 1984), there was a consensus that it was more important for providers to have appropriate values and nurturing skills than specific credentials or a specific profile regarding age, gender, or marital status. Murphy, Pennee, and Luchins (1972) pointed to the importance of the agency's attending not only to provider characteristics, but also to the location of the home. They prefer urban settings because the residents can be integrated into the community more easily, without being labeled sick or deviant. Also, they claimed, there will be a greater availability of leisure activities.

Training

According to Oktay (1987), training for foster care providers ranges from no training to training for the provision of skilled nursing care. In our first study we addressed the question of training for care providers. We found that more was provided in the way of organized training sessions by DMH than by DSS. Nevertheless, at that time training was far from extensive even in the DMH homes. When asked to recommend topics for training, the care providers in both programs suggested medication, psychology, legal concerns, personal hygiene for the residents, and information on the availability and use of community resources. Budgeting and other management issues were also mentioned as an area of training by about one-fourth of the respondents.

Since the time of our first study, the departments have put more effort into training.[1] Additionally, more attention is currently given to providing respite so that providers can attend orientation and training. The most extensive training efforts appear to be for Personal Care providers—i.e., those who care for the most disabled clients in the OMH and OMR systems. This would seem to be in

---

1. For example, since the time of the first study we have provided training for the family care providers of the DMH system. This training, involving an extensive process of needs assessment, incorporated some of the stated needs of the providers and included additional material suggested by the department. Topics were understanding the aging process; enriching the social environment; using community resources; dealing with depression; and solving problems. In addition, our Continuing Education Program has prepared for providers in the DSS system self-instructional booklets which include the following topics: special needs of the elderly, mentally ill, and mentally retarded; money management; individualized needs; food and nutrition; home safety and management; physical needs; and social needs.

line with maximizing person-environment congruence so that those residents in greatest need have the most supportive environment.

We have culled a number of training topics from the literature, from our needs assessment, and from documents about New York State. This array is by no means offered to all providers of all programs. Rather, the list can serve as a guide to what might be offered and what is needed. Such a list includes personal hygiene, exercise, body mechanics, digestion and elimination, home hazards and accident prevention, emergency assistance, medical follow-up, effects and side effects of both psychotropic and physical medication, infection control, signs of illness, vital signs, adaptive equipment, use of aids such as crutches, decubitus care, basic nutrition and special diets, mental confusion, behavioral aspects of mental illness, losses in chronic illness, gerontology, death and dying, depression, client independence, activities of daily living skills, stresses in care giving, realistic expectations, institutionalization, normalization, and interpersonal relations (Carling 1984; Oktay and Volland 1981; State of New York, OMH 1983).

Any particular training program would of course need to select its highest priorities from this list, and would offer some topics at initial training and some others at follow-up or "in-service" training. Our specific suggestions regarding family and community integration appear in the next chapter. Before leaving the topic of training, it should be emphasized that one of the major functions accompanying training is building a peer support network (Carling 1984).

Resident Selection and Matching

Here we have perhaps the most important point where the agency can enhance person-environment congruence. It is hoped that placement is according to a plan, rather than strictly according to the availability of spaces. Participants in an NIMH workshop (Carling 1984:12) included the following provider and client preferences and characteristics to be considered in matching: "personality characteristics, social interests, personal habits, gender, race, religion, cultural factors, smoking, pets, children, location, mental health/

psychiatric needs, rehabilitation needs, support service needs, medical needs, alcohol/drug problems, wheelchair accessibility." It appears that some of these are taken into consideration only through the worker's intuition, rather than through an explicit matching procedure.

Aptekar (1965) has specified that the worker is the important connecting link between the client and the home. Therefore, it might be expected that in carrying out this linkage function the worker would involve the clients and providers in creating an appropriate match. We did not find as much consultation with the providers as expected. Brearly (1977) reported a similar lack of involvement in England. Only one-quarter of the providers in our first study reported that they had ever participated in the selection of residents (they were not asked in our other two studies). The majority of the care providers indicated that they consulted with caseworkers concerning the prospective residents only at the actual time the residents were placed in their homes. This lack of participation did not always satisfy the care providers. Most providers, however, felt comfortable with their relationship with their caseworker and reported that their experience with the worker was such that the worker "knew" what type of resident the provider would want and what type would fit into the home. It is not clear how the workers knew. Perhaps more detailed assessments were made at the time the providers were accepted into the program.

Vandivort, Kurren, and Braun (1984) reported that in their program in Hawaii, the staff solicits from the provider information as to what type of client is desired. As an aid in matching clients with homes more effectively, providers in our first study were asked what traits they would look for in residents if given the chance. About one-third reported that they were looking for someone who would fit into their homes, admittedly a vague characteristic, and one-fifth indicated they would not look for any special characteristic in particular but "just someone who needs help." This means that the burden is on the caseworker to determine who would "fit in."

Three-quarters of the providers in our first study reported that they did not have a clear picture of the clients prior to their arrival. Although in most instances this lack of information was designed to protect the privacy and confidentiality of the prospective resident, at least one provider remarked that so little information was given that it was difficult to even sustain a conversation!

Although the option did not seem to be invoked frequently, caseworkers may bring the prospective resident to the foster home for a preplacement trial visit—perhaps overnight or for a weekend—to give both client and provider a chance to decide whether or not the arrangement is suitable. These visits can serve as an orientation and ease the transition for clients before they are permanently placed in the home (State of New York, Office of Mental Retardation and Developmental Disabilities 1986: 10.9.6, p. 1).

Providers in our first study agreed on the importance of preplacement visits. Some providers emphasized the value of the visits for themselves in establishing whether an individual had the qualities they were looking for in a resident. "I want to know what to expect. I fill out a form that includes medical history, hobbies, food favorites, etc." Other providers emphasized the value of such visits to prospective residents. "Trial visits are very important for residents. I want residents to know what to expect." One provider indicated that in general when people move, "you don't move right in; you go and look the place over first." Preplacement visits are also important to the residents already in the home. At least one provider remarked that it was most important for the current residents to meet and be satisfied with prospective new residents. Finally, Vandivort, Kurren, and Braun (1984) reported that not only do the provider and the client meet before placement, but relatives may also visit the prospective home. Participants in a workshop sponsored by NIMH (Carling 1984) noted the importance of involving the client's family in placement.

In some cases the providers first visit the prospective resident at the state facility. Some facilities have specific placement units that work on clients' ADL skills and prepare clients for the move. Preplacement instruction can be particularly important for residents new to foster family care.

Case Management

Following the placement of the client, the next opportunity for interaction between caseworker, care provider, and client occurs during the follow-up. Kirk and Therrien suggest that community-based services need to have "a single agency or person acting as sole agent or advocate for the patient or having primary responsibility for seeing that . . . [his] many needs are adequately met" (1975:12). Sherwood and Morris (1983) reported that the success of the domiciliary care homes (similar to family care) in their study was partially due to the case management procedures.

The Family Care team in the New York State Office of Mental Health is composed "of a multidisciplinary professional and non-professional staff, which includes a physician, nurse, social worker and/or case manager, recreation therapist, therapy aide, rehabilitation counselor, dietitian and the Family Care provider" (Carling 1984:24). Among the goals of the Family Care team in the OMH are "[assuring] the integration of the Family Care resident into the community [and providing] recreational and rehabilitative activities for the Family Care resident" (*ibid.*, p. 25). Furthermore, although health care is provided in the community, this care is arranged and monitored by Family Care nursing staff (Carling 1984). Some of the follow-up procedures in New York State have been described as follows:

Responsibility for case management, psychiatric, nursing and support services rests with the facility making the family care placement. Visits at least every month by facility family care staff are made to facilitate an integrated service plan and to monitor compliance with policy and procedures. . . . an Individual Service Plan is prepared, reviewed and revised periodically for each resident. Family care staff, the provider, the resident or someone acting on behalf of the resident, and other providers of services participate in the preparation and/or revision of the plan which includes long and short term goals, services and programs identified to meet those goals, treatment modalities and timetables for attainment. (State of New York, OMH 1983:28)

Similar to the OMH program, the Office of Mental Retardation and Developmental Disabilities also spells out a plan for placement and follow-up:

It is the responsibility of the Program Planning Team to: provide appropriate assessments on at least an annual basis; identify the client's needs; design a comprehensive plan of care; provide programs and services in accordance with the plan; periodically review the client's progress and the plan of care in response to the client's changing needs; ensure that the client's services and activities in both the Family Care Home and the day program/activity are compatible and are being provided in accordance with the plan of care; [make] necessary changes in the plan of care. [The Family Care case manager is] responsible for reviewing and supervising each client's program and for coordinating the inputs and assignments of other professionals and disciplines. (State of New York, OMR 1986: 10.7.2, p. 1)

Each client and each home must be visited at least monthly (*ibid.*, 10.8.6 and 7).

Other programs also place an emphasis on staff follow-up. Vandivort, Kurren, and Braun (1984) consider the first three months crucial in this process. Oktay and Volland (1981), in describing a family care program for the frail elderly in Baltimore, also point to an adjustment period in the early months necessitating extensive supportive services. They mention the importance of respite care services and group meetings for providers.

In our first study (DSS and DMH) we asked providers about follow-up services they had received (not asked in the second or third studies). Results indicated that follow-up procedures and the frequency of personal visits by caseworkers varied greatly. Eighty percent of the providers in the DMH program reported weekly or monthly visits by caseworkers. "We have constant contact; we're not out in left field," one provider commented. "The hospital works with me. They would never refuse anything. They would never ignore you. I get fast results from the agency," commented another. "The social workers really care about the residents, and are very supportive. They know the residents by name and are aware of their histories without looking it up in their files," said a third.

In contrast to the 80 percent reported by DMH providers, only about one-quarter of those in the DSS program reported weekly or monthly follow-up visits. Almost half the DSS care providers reported follow-up visits taking place less than three times per year. However, it was found that those who received less frequent visits were as likely to consider the visits sufficient as those who received more frequent visits. It may be that the DSS clients had fewer problems and were perceived to require less follow-up than the DMH residents. "DSS was coming too often. I didn't feel I needed any help and told her to stop coming. She only comes once a year now."

Providers indicated that the quality of follow-up visits was more important than the quantity. Providers also indicated that the main impact of the caseworker was not experienced through repeated home visits but through his or her availability if and when a problem arose. As one provider stated, "It's important to know they can be reached by phone when we need them."

About two-thirds of the providers felt that personal follow-ups were beneficial to both residents and provider. Occasionally the visits were seen as an intrusion. For example, one provider exclaimed, "The less the better—they are a pain in the neck." Those who felt the visits were not beneficial gave two reasons: the workers were more concerned with enforcing regulations than with residents' needs, and the residents were fearful that they would be removed from the home when they saw the worker—either because the home did not meet standards, or because they themselves did not meet some standard. The residents' concern should be subject to alleviation at least in part by some explanations by the provider and caseworker.

Caseworkers who were interested only in the physical makeup of the house and the medical records of the residents were not seen as helpful; those workers who displayed interest in the residents and their problems were seen as most helpful by the providers. Recent changes of the New York State Office of Mental Retardation and Developmental Disabilities have decentralized the "quality assurance function." This is thought to be more "homelike" (Lin 1987). Conformity with regulations is assessed in a nonthreatening way by the caseworker on her regular visits. Oktay and Volland (1981) also pointed to the need for flexibility on the case manager's part, so that the family nature of the homes is preserved. This sometimes involves compromises on rules and regulations if the patient's needs and preferences are to be respected.

DISCUSSION

Most of the providers in our studies had been recruited by other providers, either friends or family. It would appear that the agencies themselves could be more active in this area, although additional staff might be required not only to do the recruiting but to screen, train, and supervise these newcomers. Foster family care for adults is a program that is not generally known to the public, and the agencies might expand their current public education activities. In addition to acting as a mechanism to recruit providers, this kind of information would provide an additional option for families looking for solutions to the care of dependent adults and might help to convince the elderly themselves of the efficacy of sharing their lives with others and not to view foster care as relinquishing independence.

By and large, the care providers claimed to be motivated chiefly by their desire to work with people rather than primarily by the desire to supplement their income. In fact, agency personnel tried to eliminate applicants who were "more interested in money than in helping." The care providers in all three of our studies appeared to be genuinely interested in the welfare of their residents, and providers indicated that they would like to be more active participants in the selection of their residents. Although they understood the departmental regulations designed to protect the privacy of their residents, particularly in regard to their past history and medications, many providers felt the relationship between them and their residents could be helped if the caseworkers offered them more information about the prospective clients.

An additional factor to enhance morale, as expressed by providers, is the availability of agency personnel not only for basic support but especially for emergency calls. Providers also expressed opinions about the role of the caseworker and follow-up visits. They felt that the caseworker should act primarily as an advocate for the client. Providers urged going beyond mere checking to see that the homes met the standards as set down by the departments to include more emphasis on the quality of life of the foster home residents and their interpersonal relationships. The providers' composite picture of the ideal caseworker was one who would give the care provider a useful description of the prospective resident, present a clear picture of the foster home to the resident, follow up on placements, and be readily available when problems arose.

As a final note, the providers in our first study, more than half of whom already belonged to such an association, felt that an association of care providers enhances morale by providing an exchange of information and a vehicle for training, and serving a social function for both providers and residents. An association also can enhance development by exerting an influence upon program planners.

A possible direction for future efforts in strengthening adult foster care programs is to focus on the interaction among the provider, resident, and caseworker. In order to make this interaction more positive and productive, caseworkers need a clear understanding of their own role and of the expectations held by the agency, as well as by the care provider and resident. We turn in the next chapter to recommendations and policy directions for the future.

Summary: This chapter has described the distinct roles played by each actor in foster family care. The provider brings special skills (that may need enhancement through training) and, in particular, a very special caring for dependent persons. She appears to be motivated by a desire to help, as well as by a desire for companionship. She needs to be assisted to turn this into mature caring. Most of the providers in our studies had been recruited by other providers, either friends or family. The provider plays an important role as a facilitator of community integration. The resident brings special competencies and demands, frequently a lifetime of dependency, perhaps even of institutionalization. For most of the older residents of all three programs, foster care is not typically a way station toward greater independence but, rather, the last stop before a skilled nursing facility or death. Foster care is home for these people, and the roles and relationships in which they engage in the home are the focus of their lives. The role of the client's "natural family" was minimal, and in some cases attention by the relatives was seen as dysfunctional by the provider. However, the relatives' role might be expanded in other cases. And finally, agency personnel bring the other actors together through the processes of recruitment and selection of homes, training, client selection and matching, and ongoing case management of foster placements.

6 · Conclusions And Recommendations

In recent years community alternatives in long-term care for older persons have assumed increasing importance for both economic and social reasons. Increasing expenses associated with institutional care and the suggestion that care in the community is more "humane" than care in an institution have caused policy and program planners to seek alternative services. One form of alternative service is foster family care. Adult foster care is a complex, multifaceted phenomenon. Foster family residents and providers are older than the public might generally have believed. Although the primary benefit of foster family care is its familial nature, this aspect is not always automatic and needs concerted effort and training. An additional benefit is integration into the community, also requiring deliberate action on the part of the provider.

Foster family care for adults is widespread both temporally and spatially, i.e., it is one of the oldest forms of care, beginning centuries ago, and it exists across this country and in other countries as well. Yet it has received relatively little research attention. Although the literature uses a variety of terms for this form of care, and although foster care and family care have different histories and different sponsoring agencies, many of the principles of care are the same. In this book, foster family care is used to designate the placement of no more than about six clients, and typically one to three, with a private family or individual, for supportive care and ongoing supervision by an agency.

As we have described earlier in this book, for dependent older persons, foster family care is not usually a step toward greater independence, but frequently a last stop before a skilled nursing facility or death. It may shorten hospital stays and keep people out of nursing homes for a time. It may also help to prevent reinstitutionalization. Some view foster care as a custodial placement for chronic individuals who have reached a plateau or are gradually deteriorating. Others see it as a therapeutic environment. Still others view it as a transitional facility between the dependence of the institution and independence in the community.

It is our conclusion that almost any foster care program can be therapeutic. The arena for the therapy may differ among clients; i.e., the focus of attention may be the family or the community, in some cases both. Although residents may not be able to move to independent living, some may still improve in their functional level, given the proper stimulation and attention. Foster family care for adults should not be used as it sometimes has been in the past so that one can "forget about" persons and have no further expectations of them. Foster family care has the potential to maximize the person's skills and to facilitate adaptation by adjusting the demands upward or downward to fit the person's changing competence levels.

Proponents of foster family care contend that adult residents will benefit from integration into the life of the family and the larger community. Our studies have examined the factors that contribute to making foster care a viable option for three adult groups: the mentally ill, the mentally retarded, and the frail elderly. Some of the recommendations we make have already been implemented in the specific programs we studied, partially as a result of our early recommendations. We present them as general recommendations that can be applied in any locale.

The extent to which foster family care for adults is truly familial has been debated extensively. The debate has ranged from the claim that foster family care provides a surrogate family to the claim that foster family care is no more than a mini-institution. Our research leads us to suggest that foster family care has the potential for making the provider and residents a true family. With respect to community integration, the picture is more complicated. We suggest that a more precise delineation of community integration is needed. It is essential to distinguish community acceptance from community participation, and to have realistic goals for community integration, both with and without the care provider.

FAMILY INTEGRATION

In the words of one of the providers we interviewed: "We should keep the small homes. In the big ones, you're a number, not a name. You get to know each other in small homes." While acknowledging that some of the arguments for small homes are impressionistic, rather than research based, many would agree with Morrissey's (1967) explanation that the small number of people encountered in the family care home affords the opportunity for the development of relationships among residents and between care providers and residents. Because of their vulnerability, the residents of foster care are particularly affected by the environment. In this setting it is possible for intense, one-to-one relationships to be formed between care providers and residents, and at times among the residents themselves. Smaller size also affords more opportunity for spontaneity. Large institutions require more formal programmed activities, without a great deal of leeway to promote individual differences.

In addition to the size of the home, an important consideration is the issue of regulation. Oktay (1987) indicates that at present there are no uniform licensing standards in adult foster care. It is critical to protect the client from abuse or neglect. On the other hand, we conclude from our studies that protection should not result in over-regulation. It is important that the essence of the family climate not be destroyed, nor potential providers discouraged from applying (see also Linn 1981; and Mor, Sherwood, and Gutkin 1986). The staff monitoring the homes need to understand that it is the very informality and lack of regidity that present the homes with their unique advantages. For example, meals may not always be served at the same time, or according to a dietitian's standards; they might be served when the client is hungry, and fit the client's tastes (see also Oktay and Volland 1981). While standards of cleanliness must be maintained, a degree of "untidiness" may not only be tolerable, but even be desirable.

Providers told us the caseworker should act primarily as an advocate for the client, rather than strictly as an enforcer of the rules, and should place more emphasis on the quality of life of the client. Since there seems to be a working informal relationship between providers and caseworkers, written regulations might simply be guidelines within which the worker can help the "family" nature to flourish, rather than rigid rules for conformity. Providers should be selected who are able to maintain a good relationship with the agency. The ideal caseworker from the point of view of the provider is one who gives a clear picture of the resident before the placement, who is available when needed, and who is flexible. It is important for the agency to afford the caseworker this kind of role. It is perhaps easier for the caseworker to enforce rules than to act as facilitator of familism. Thus caseworkers can benefit from training for their role.

Expectations should be communicated to the care providers regarding family interaction. In particular, providers might need further training to guide them toward treating the residents as adults, rather than acting maternalistically. For some, this new way of thinking will require continual reinforcement. Training should be both preliminary to the placement and "in-service"—during early phases of the placement and periodically throughout the placement. Training can be both formal, in groups, and informal, during individual visits by caseworkers. One of the advantages of group training is that providers can share with others with similar concerns (Sherman, Newman, and Kucij 1981). The Family Care Association meetings could serve as a vehicle for training, interaction, and mutual understanding for both care provider and caseworker.

Residents need to share at least some common space in the house with the provider and her family, so that conversation and sociability are learned and practiced, and so that trust is engendered and maintained. Providers should be selected who do not mind some loss of their own privacy. Adjustment should be enhanced by allowing the resident power over her own decisions whenever possible. Although the environment permits individualized treatment and tolerance for deviance, residents long institutionalized should be trained in socialization skills. A "high expectation philosophy" emphasizing strength, not illness (Richmond 1971:119), is recommended.

Decisions about resident participation in chores appear to be based on age and perceived ability, as well as the provider's convenience in some cases. The Lawton and Nahemow (1973) framework would predict negative outcomes when a resident who has the competence to do some minor chores or prepare a snack is not permitted to do so because it inconveniences the provider. Training would help to increase the tolerance of the provider, extend the capabilities and reduce the frustrations of the resident, and distinguish between beneficial experiences for the resident and exploitation. The resident needs to know what is expected. Help with chores should be part of a specific plan, worked out with the caseworker. The caseworker would monitor the home so that the resident is not used to excess—exploited for the convenience of the provider (State of New York, OMR 1986: 10.6.3 [rev.], p. 1).

Family care is in a position to raise the individual's level of competence and to augment demand and should aim for the proper balance between "maximizing motivation for exercise of skills" and "overstepping the individual's limits of tolerance for stress" (Lawton and Nahemow 1973). An example of raising competence would be stimulating the resident to relearn skills necessary for daily interpersonal interaction, such as personal grooming. Raising the demands to increase challenge can, for example, mean urging the resident to venture out into the neighborhood, or at least to eat dinner with the family.

Foster family care also might be used more extensively as a benefit to the care provider herself. A "traditional" family may not be necessary. Many of the best homes proved to be those in which the provider had no other relatives in the household. Being a family care provider can provide persons who are themselves in their fifties and older and who are living with no natural family of their own a great deal of personal satisfaction and a meaningful role in their later years. This might be particularly important for widows. The provider and the resident can be seen in reciprocal roles, each fulfilling her needs for adult attachment (Bowlby 1969; Sable 1979).

The congruence between personal needs and the environment's ability to fulfill those needs is high for the provider as well as for the resident.

At the same time, the issue of inappropriate dependency upon the provider needs to be addressed. The provider must be thought of in the role of a facilitator of independence, not as one who encourages dependency. In some cases, the provider is in the program primarily because she herself needs companionship. While this is not to be discouraged, the needs and growth of the primary client must be served. Here the caseworker can be most useful in mediating between the needs of residents for independence and the needs of the provider for companionship.

Both internal (family) and external (community) integration are important goals. Segal and Aviram (1978) describe internal integration as an avenue for the development of supportive relationships. The development of such relationships is gratifying and should be seen as an end in and of itself. Additionally, the family system can serve as an essential link between the individual and community; we will discuss this next.

COMMUNITY INTEGRATION

Community integration is a major goal of family care, both as an important aspect of normalization and as a vehicle for the learning or relearning of daily living and social skills (Kultgen and Habenstein 1981). However, community integration has been only vaguely defined and therefore inconsistently evaluated. In our studies we operationally defined integration as incorporating both community acceptance and community participation.

From the point of view of community acceptance, foster family care appears to show promise. Much has been written attributing the failure of the integration of deinstitutionalized persons to community opposition, stigmatization, and nontolerance of deviance. One hypothesis of our study was that because of the relatively small size and familiarity of a family care home, there would be little opposition to this setting. This was confirmed by our data. According to both residents and care providers, the level of acceptance of the family care residents is high. It appears that these small homes are less obtrusive in the community, and the residents are not seen as a threat. The provider who is an accepted community resident appears to be able to facilitate entry into the community without arousing hostility. It is still questionable, however, whether receptivity in specific programs, e.g., senior citizens centers, is as high as the general acceptance of the home in the neighborhood.

Although the level of acceptance by neighbors was high, a concomitantly high level of resident participation in the community was not observed. To some extent the life of family care residents in the community appeared to be marginal rather than integral; their use of resources, a passive consumptive role (Segal and Aviram 1978), was much higher than participation in formal or informal activities and socializing. If we compare the frequency of participation in psychiatric/developmental center activities with the frequency of participation in other activities, we find that the former is substantially higher. Likewise, neighbors might be better described as acquaintances than as friends.

While the residents' participation may represent a superficial involvement in community life, family care residents are not merely residing in the community and dependent on the sheltered subsociety that Lamb and Goertzel (1971) claim former patients often find and choose. In addition to their integration into a family unit, to varying degrees they are integrated into the foster family's network of relatives, neighbors, and friends. Family care residents thus appear to represent a midpoint on the continuum of isolation versus integration into the community. They are clearly not isolated; they have available to them the supports of the family care home and a degree of external integration. On the other hand, they are not active participants in the life of their communities.

Results of a study such as this dealing with the impaired older adult must be viewed not in absolute terms, but relative to realistic expectations regarding the population. We have used as a comparison the participation level of their family care providers. Perhaps more realistically, community participation should be compared with the levels of integration found among similar persons who reside in institutions, or in other special residences in the community, or with relatives, or alone. For example, we find that the level of reported activity of foster care residents is higher than that described in other types of living arrangements with comparable populations (e.g., David, Moos, and Kahn 1981; Horizon House 1975; Segal and Aviram 1978). Further, much of the literature on similar living arrangements does not include persons as old as some of those in our sample.

It is now recognized that not all residents have the potential to move out of family care to live more independently. In the same way, expectations of community integration while in family care may need a more realistic reappraisal. The agencies placing elderly adults in foster family care must determine what is meant by "participation in the life of the community." Integration may best be understood not in global terms, but rather in terms of focused goals based on the ability and desires of each resident.

It is important that each resident be encouraged to participate to the greatest degree possible. It is also critical, however, to assess realistically each client's potential for integration and where that is low, to provide rewarding interactions within the range of the person's limitations—a particular strength of family care. It is vital that the treatment plan carefully spells out capabilities, expectations, and methods for achieving greater independence. It is most important to recognize, however, that this plan has to be revised frequently as many of the frail elderly residents will show more decline than progress toward independence. The emphasis needs to be at all times on maximizing the skills available.

It is evident that the care provider plays a key role in effecting family and community integration. Clearly, the creation of home environments that are conducive to family integration are to a large extent dependent on the care provider. The data presented here, however, point to an additional role for the care provider, that of a facilitator of community integration. Our data suggest that many family care residents, particularly those placed through the Office of Mental Retardation and Developmental Disabilities, are dependent on their care providers for much of their participation in activities.

Because of the provider's importance in the resident's community participation, it is necessary to know the nature of the provider's own participation in community life. Questions need to be raised about the use of providers whose own social skills are marginal.

Additionally, program managers need to think carefully about the relative merits of participation with and without the care provider. On the one hand, participation along with the care provider can facilitate integration into the community in two ways. For residents it serves to extend the security of the home into the unfamiliar and perhaps frightening community environment. For members of the community, it provides a familiar frame of reference through which they can meet the stranger. On the other hand, participation without the provider signifies that some level of independence has been reached. Participation without the provider also enables the resident to enjoy activities in which the provider may not be interested or for which the provider may not have time.

When selecting both the homes and the clients, a major objective is to achieve the best possible congruence between the person and the environment. This study has demonstrated the need to assess each client and each provider to determine the proper match between them. Both in recruitment and training, providers should be sought who participate actively in the community and who through training can be encouraged to include residents in their activities. Care providers would benefit from training that would help them capitalize on the strengths they can provide as facilitators of participation in the community. Training would also help care providers to assess their own needs to be overprotective when residents are able to socialize and participate either alone or with other residents without the presence of the care provider.

In the selection of an adult foster care home, the issue of the number of residents as it relates to community integration is complex and depends on goals. In the OMH homes we studied, the number of residents was negatively associated with socialization and activities with the provider; in the OMR homes we studied, the number of residents was positively associated with socialization and activities without the provider. We might speculate that taken together these results suggest that if there are too many residents, the provider finds it difficult to take them into the community, and if there is a "critical mass" of residents, they can go into the community on their own. If community resources are not available, small homes may not be beneficial. It may be desirable in those instances to place residents in homes that contain enough residents so they can provide socialization, entertainment, and companionship for each other while still resembling a "family," and not a mini-institution.

We should not idealize the small size of family care per se. Some have commented that the smallness of foster care does not offer sufficient benefit to justify the sparseness of services—services that might be available within larger residences. Recreational and social services should be available in the community. Rather than enlarging individual homes, in some cases it could be advantageous for several homes to combine resources in order to maximize what they can offer. Particular attention must be given to those homes in rural areas. The associations of care providers may provide group activities for residents. Perhaps most important, however, increased attention needs to be given to integrating foster family care with other community services for the elderly, such as day care, respite, senior centers, and congregate meals. The residents of family care need to be given the skills so they will be welcome, and the staff and members of these community programs need to be educated to be more receptive.

FUTURE RESEARCH

Although adult foster care has a long history, we believe its full potential has yet to be tapped. If this potential is to be realized, certain questions still need to be answered. Some of these are the following:

- Attention to the "mix" or modal characteristics of the residents, i.e., the advantages and disadvantages of sex, age, or ability integration as they affect family and community integration. Related to this is the question of whether it is advantageous for the group of family care residents to use community resources as a group. They provide mutual support, but traveling as a group may exaggerate their "differentness," and may, in fact, discourage the development of independence.
- Clarification of the direction of causality regarding community integration. Is the relatively low level of community participation a function of residents' fears and reluctance to develop new relationships, or inexperience in performing these activities? Or is it rather a manifestation of informal methods of exclusion used by

the community to deal with deviants (Aviram and Segal 1973), or a lack of attractive activities or transportation? A study could be conducted to assess directly the attitudes of community members. Perhaps if the provider is not active in the community, residents conform to this model. What can be done to increase participation?

- A study of records to discriminate the characteristics of those providers who remain from those who drop out of foster family care. This needs to be examined in conjunction with characteristics of residents to help determine if one reason for dropout is a poor match between resident and provider. How can predictions of a good match be improved?
- An observational study of the pattern of daily activities, including a more detailed look at the physical configuration and use of the home (Lawton 1984). Representative homes could be chosen and studied intensively.

FUTURE DEVELOPMENT OF FOSTER FAMILY CARE

According to current demographic predictions, there will continue to be a need for family care for mentally ill and developmentally disabled older persons. The New York State Office of Mental Health, for example, has pointed to the prevalence of "depression and other psychiatric disorders serious enough to require personal care in the activities of daily living" (State of New York, OMH 1986:86). The need for family care in the Mental Retardation and Developmental Disabilities system is increasing because the natural family is aging. That is, even if the client was able to live with parents as a young adult, by the time the mentally retarded person has reached middle age, it is likely that his or her parents will have died, or become unable to continue caring for him or her, because of the parents' own frailties. Seeing the adult child make the transition into foster care can be reassuring to parents. The knowledge that family life and a sense of stability will go on without a need for institutionalization can also alleviate fears held by the disabled person.

Policymakers and planners have become increasingly aware of the backup of frail elderly persons in acute care hospitals because they have no one to whom they can be discharged. The use of foster family care for the elderly as a preventative alternative could be increased when it becomes apparent that soon the person will be unable to meet the demands of an independent setting, but before there is a need for the higher levels of care offered in a nursing facility.

Program administrators from all three programs in our study predicted an increase in the need for adult family care in the future, particularly for the older client. They judged that many of the residents would have had to go into a long-term care facility if it were not for family care. At the time of this writing all three agencies have been engaged in attempts to stabilize and expand family care. For example, the Office of Mental Health has targeted approximately a 40 percent increase in family care placements over a ten-year period (State of New York, OMH 1986:3).

In an effort to increase the size of the program and perhaps to find homes for those hard to place, the departments involved in foster family care are making attempts to increase the recruitment of providers and keep those they now have. Some of these initiatives that are beneficial to both residents and care providers are increased SSI payment levels for family care residents, increased payment for providers, decentralization and simplification of regulations to reflect the family nature of the homes, use of community mental health centers or other voluntary agencies as the sponsoring agency, funding for special needs such as clothing, transportation to recreational and cultural activities (e.g., museums, amusement parks, or other field trips), and increased respite care so the provider may attend orientation or training, go on vacation, or take care of personal needs (Lin 1987; Plummer 1986; State of New York, Department of Social Services, August 16, 1985; State of New York, DSS November 15, 1985; State of New York, OMH 1986; State of New York, OMR 1986).

Foster care for adults is a program that is not generally known to the public, and the agencies must expand their current public education activities. In particular, they need to distinguish foster homes from unsupervised options such as board and care homes. Efforts must be made to reduce the stigma associated with the use of foster family care. Increased public awareness will help not only to recruit providers, but will enable prospective residents and their relatives to be aware of foster care as an option.

While foster family care historically has been used primarily for mentally ill and mentally retarded persons, it is our contention that it could and should be used more extensively by the frail elderly, with a range of economic needs. At the present time it appears that referral mechanisms are generally better established for those older adults in the mental health or mental retardation systems than for the community elderly without a history of mental problems or involvement with social agencies. Perhaps this is true because funding mechanisms are better established in the former. We need to have better case-finding and placement processes for those frail elderly who are in the community, at risk of institutionalization or of isolation without needed support. If the program is to be viable, questions of funding the program for those not currently in the service system must be faced. Funding sources for adult foster care vary, the most typical being the resident's own resources, SSI benefits, VA pensions, and recently, in some cases, Medicaid (Oktay 1987). Costs paid to care providers, however, represent only a portion of the expenses and exclude administrative costs. This might be an area of growth for the private nonprofit market.

We have studied 352 homes located across New York State, sponsored by three agencies, and housing approximately 1,150 residents. Our belief, based on our review of the literature, on our application of social science theory, and on the universality of questions of family and community, is that our findings and recommendations are generalizable to other locations. As described by one of the program administrators interviewed in our first study, family care "avoids institutionalization and provides a system of follow-up that compels visibility of services to the individual, at times provides hope and motivation for something better, a fuller life-style, and in some instances, a home life never before realized. It offers freer access to normalization and the tempo of true community life."

Appendix 1 · Sample Care Provider Interview

INTERVIEWER

Does the neighborhood in which the home is located consist of:
— Farmhouses
— Single-family homes
— Combination of single-family homes, duplexes, apartments
— Apartment houses
— Combination of stores, businesses, and residential dwellings
— Primarily stores and businesses
— Primarily warehouses and factories
— Other. Describe: _____

_____

Is the neighborhood in which the home is located:
— Rural—sparsely populated with a fair amount of farming or open land.
— Urban—houses have small or no yards, and the preponderance of structures are multifamily housing apartments or commercial structures.
— Suburban—houses are quite close together but maintain separate yards, and there are few or no large tracts of open lands or farms.

—Other. Describe: _____

_____

Sex of respondent:
—male
—female

_____

[The Interview Begins]

First I'd like to ask you some questions about this neighborhood
or area.

1. Does the community within which your home is located have
a public transportation system?
   No -- GO TO QUESTION 3
┌─Yes
└▶2. Is there a public transportation stop within easy walking dis-
   tance of your home? (2–3 blocks)
   Yes
   No

```
┌─────────────────────────────────────────────────────────┐
│                        Card A                            │
│                                                          │
│  (1) Must have private transportation                    │
│  (2) Can use public transportation                       │
│  (3) Can walk but it's a good long walk                  │
│  (4) Within easy walking distance                        │
│  (5) Both 2 and 3                                        │
│  (0) Other. Please explain: _____         │
└─────────────────────────────────────────────────────────┘
```

3. Using the choices on this card (PRESENT CARD A), please tell me
   how convenient it is to get to . . .
   A shopping center or local shopping area
4. A park
5. A library
6. A movie theater
7. A community center (e.g., YMCA or senior center)
8. A restaurant or coffee shop

9. A bar
10. A place of worship which would meet the religious needs of some of your residents
11. An organization that offers individuals an opportunity to do volunteer work
12. A barbershop or beauty shop

13. How safe do you feel being *out alone* in your neighborhood or area?
    Very safe
    Somewhat safe
    Somewhat unsafe
    Very unsafe
14. How would you describe the ethnic background of most of the people in your neighborhood or area?

Black	Other: East European
Italian-American	_____
Irish-American	(which?)
Hispanic-American	Other: West European
Polish-American	_____
Native American/Indian	(which?)
	Other: Asian
	_____
	(which?)
	American
	Other: _____
	(which?)

15. How long have you lived at this address?
    Less than one year
    1 year or more but less than 5 years
    5 years or more but less than 10 years
    10 years or more but less than 20 years   SKIP TO
    20 years or more _____ QUESTION 17

    If Less Than 10 Years at Same Address, Ask:

16. How long have you lived in this neighborhood or area?
    Less than one year
    1 year or more but less than 5 years

    5 years or more but less than 10 years
    10 years or more but less than 20 years
    20 years or more

17. Are there other members of your family living in your home? (check all that apply)

None	Children over age 10
Spouse	Elderly relatives
Children under age 10	Others: Who? _____

I am going to ask you about some activities you might participate in. For each activity please look at this card (PRESENT CARD B) and tell me which category *best* describes how frequently you participate.

Card B

Once a day	Several times a year
2–6 times a week	Once a year or less
Once a week	
2–3 times a month	
Once a month	

---

18. About how frequently do you spend some time with any of your neighbors? That is, how often do you go to see them, or they come to see you, or you go out to do things together?
19. About how frequently do you spend some time with friends from outside the home? That is, how often do you go to see them, or they come to see you, or you go out to do things together?
20. About how frequently do you spend some time with any of your relatives? That is, how often do you go out to see them, or they come to see you or you go to do things together?
21. How often do you go to some meeting place such as a bar, park, ice cream shop?
22. How often do you go on a picnic?
23. How often do you go to a ball game or other sports event?
24. How often do you attend religious services?

25. How often do you attend funerals, weddings, or other such ceremonies?
26. How often do you eat in a restaurant?
27. How often do you attend a concert or play?
28. How often do you attend the movies?
29. How often do you go to parties?
30. How often do you engage in volunteer work?
31. How often do you go to clubs or community or senior citizens centers?

Now I have some questions about the family care residents in your home.

32. How many residents do you have living in your home at this time? _____

I will read you the names of people who are recorded to have been living in your home a few months ago. Please tell me if any are no longer living with you. Have any new people moved in? Please give me their names and ages.

As you know, _____ is participating in our study and so I will ask you some questions about him/her.

33. How long ago did ____ _____ first come to live in your home?
    Less than 6 months
    6 months to one year
    1–2 years
    2–5 years
    More than 5 years. How many? _____
34. Has _____ lived outside your home during the past year? If YES: Where?
    No _____ GO TO QUESTION 36
    In hospital
    In psychiatric center
    Visited friend
    Visited relative
    Other, describe: _____
35. For how long did _____ live there?

Less than one week
1–2 weeks
More than 2 weeks–less than 1 month
More than 1 month–less than 6 months
More than 6 months
Left a number of times; explain: _____

36. How long do you anticipate _____ will stay in your home?
Short-term (temporary)
Long-term
Permanent

37. Is _____ currently employed?
No
Full-time
Part-time
Sporadically
Sheltered workshop
Volunteer work

38. What ethnic group does _____ feel closest to?

Black	Other: West European
Italian-American	_____
Irish-American	(which?)
Hispanic-American	Other: Asian _____
Polish-American	(which?)
Native American/Indian	American
Other: East European	Other: _____
_____	(which?)
(which)?	

I am going to ask you some questions about _____'s ability to do things by him/herself.

For each task please tell me whether _____ generally does it, whether he/she is capable of doing it, and whether he/she generally did it at the time when he/she came to live with you. (PRESENT CARD C.) You can use this card to help you answer.

Card C

No
With reminders
Independently
Don't know

---

39. Takes care of his/her own appearance—that is, dresses neatly and appropriately
40. Generally knows what day and month it is
41. Uses socially acceptable table manners
42. Gets around the neighborhood without getting confused
43. Handles his/her own spending money
44. Knows basic current events
45. Uses the telephone
46. Has a sense of responsibility toward own or provider's possessions
47. Has a sense of responsibility toward others
48. Follows a schedule (that is, shows up for meals and scheduled activities)
49. Carries on a conversation
50. Initiates a conversation
51. Makes decisions
52. Uses the bus system
53. Does shopping
54. Is _____ withdrawn?

    Never
    Rarely
    Sometimes
    Often
    Always

    (QUESTIONS 55–61 USE SAME ALTERNATIVES.)

55. Is _____ 's thinking confused, disorganized?
56. Is _____ depressed?
57. Does _____ overreact emotionally?

58. Does _____ underreact emotionally?
59. Is _____ suspicious?
60. Is _____ hostile?
61. Does _____ say very strange or bi-
    zarre things in public? or exhibit strange behavior in public?
62. Has _____ met the neighbors? How?
    No
    Yes, on own initiative
    Yes, provider introduced
    Yes, other. How? _____
63. Has _____ been invited into your
    neighbors' homes?
    No
    Rarely
    Sometimes
    Often
64. Is _____ reluctant to meet and inter-
    act with neighbors or other people in your neighborhood or
    area?
    Yes
    No
65. Could you tell me what kinds of things you do to encourage
    _____ to go out and spend time in the
    community?

    _____

    Nothing
    Transport to community support services
       or psychiatric center programs
    Transport to community resources
    Transport to allow visits
    Take him/her with me when I go out
       to shop, movies, restaurant, church, etc.
    Take him/her with me when I go visiting
    Introduce him/her to friends, neighbors
    Arrange (help arrange) for him/her to go to centers or meet
       with friends
    Other

    _____

I'll give you this card (PRESENT CARD B) back again. This time, please tell me how often _____ participates in each of these activities. Tell how often he/she participates *without* you and how often *with* you.

Card B

Once a day	Several times a year
2–6 times a week	Once a year or less
Once a week	
2–3 times a month	
Once a month	

INTERVIEWER: RATE EACH ACTIVITY TWICE; ONCE WITHOUT PROVIDER AND ONCE WITH PROVIDER.

66. About how frequently does _____ _____ spend some time with any of your neighbors? That is, how often does he/she go to see them, or they come to see him/her, or they go out to do things together?
67. About how frequently does _____ spend some time with friends from outside the home? That is, how often does he/she go to see him/her, or they go out to do things together?
68. About how frequently does _____ spend some time with any of his/her relatives? That is, how often does he/she do out to see them, or they come to see him/her or they go to do things together?
69. How often does she/he go to some meeting place such as a bar, park, ice cream shop?
70. How often does she/he go to a picnic?
71. How often does she/he go to a ball game or other sports event?
72. How often does she/he attend religious services?
73. How often does she/he attend funerals, weddings, or other such ceremonies?
74. How often does she/he eat in a restaurant?
75. How often does she/he attend a concert or play?
76. How often does she/he attend the movies?

77. How often does she/he go to parties?
78. How often does she/he engage in volunteer work?
79. How often does she/he go to clubs or community or senior citizens centers?
80. How often does _____ participate in activities either at the psychiatric center or sponsored by the psychiatric center?
   (PROBE: such as vocational training, sheltered workshop, day program, meals, social club, or therapy group)
81. Does _____ generally use any of the following services in the community?
   Yes
   No
   The service is not available in the community
   (1) Doctor (other than from psychiatric facility)
   (2) Dentist
   (3) Hairdresser or barber
   (4) Post office
   (5) Public transportation
   (6) Drugstore
   (7) Grocery
82. How would you say your neighbors generally respond to ____
   _____ ? (READ ALTERNATIVES)
   Generally friendly
   Indifferent (cold, businesslike)
   Hostile or annoyed
   Warm and accepting
   Avoid him/her
      DON'T READ
   Mixed, describe: _____
   Other, describe: _____
83. When _____ appears in a public place like church or local shops, how would you say people respond?
   Are they (READ ALTERNATIVES)
   Generally friendly
   Indifferent (cold, businesslike)
   Hostile or annoyed
   Warm and accepting

Avoid him/her
  DON'T READ
Mixed, describe: _____
Other, describe: _____

84. Have there been any particularly positive or favorable incidents
in the neighborhood or area with regard to _____ ?
Yes
No -- GO TO QUESTION 86
85. If yes, explain: _____

86. Have there been any particularly negative or unfavorable incidents in the neighborhood or area with regard to _____
_____ ?

Yes
No --- GO TO QUESTION 88
87. If yes, explain: _____ _____

Now I'm going to ask you some questions about all your residents,
not just about _____.

88. Have there been any complaints about your family care home?
Yes, explain: _____
No

Here is a card describing possible attitudes people may have about
having a family care home in the neighborhood.

Card D
Most unfavorable
Somewhat unfavorable
Neutral
Somewhat favorable
Most favorable

89. How would you rate the way you think your neighbors feel
about having a family care home for adults in this neighborhood? (Use Card D.)

90. On the same scale, how do you think the storekeepers and other business people in this neighborhood or area feel about having a family care home for adults in the neighborhood?

91. Among your residents, how often are close friendships formed?
    Never Always
    Rarely Never has more than one resident
    Sometimes
    Often

92. Do you ever find yourself forming close friendships with the residents? If *yes*, how often does this happen?
    Never Often
    Rarely Always
    Sometimes

93. How often do the residents eat *at least* one meal a day with the family?
    Never Always
    Rarely Mixed, describe:
    Sometimes _____
    Often

94. Excluding bedrooms, are certain parts of your home reserved for just your own family or just the residents?
    All rooms used by all
    Sections for family only—others common
    Sections for residents only—others common
    Some sections for each—others common

Now I just have a few more questions about yourself, just for statistical purposes.

95. Are you now:
    Married
    Single/never married
    Divorced/separated
    Widowed

96. What is the highest grade of school you completed?
    1st through 6th grade College, some
    7th through 9th grade College, completed
    10th through 12th grade Other, specify: _____

97. What is your religion?
    Protestant
    Catholic
    Jewish
    Other, specify: _____
    None

98. What ethnic group do you feel closest to? (READ ALL IF NEEDED)
    Black   Other: East European
    Italian-American
    Jewish-American   _____
    Hispanic-American   (which?)
    Polish-American   Other: West European
    Native American/Indian
                             _____
                                         (which?)
                             Other: Asian _____
                                           (which?)
                             American
                             Other: _____
                                         (which?)

99. How old were you on your last birthday? _____

Thank you for your cooperation.

Please note any problems or information not covered in the
interview: ____ _____

Appendix 2 · Sampling Frames and Response Rates

In study 1, conducted in 1976, homes had to have at least one resident aged 60 or over to be in the sample. The response rate was 97 percent (3 refusals out of 103 attempts). Care providers were asked to respond to some questions separately for each resident 60 or older in the home. For these items, therefore, in the 50 DSS homes we have data on 135 residents, and in the 50 DMH homes we have data on 97 residents.

In study 2, conducted in 1981, homes from both the urban and rural sites were stratified by age of the residents (obtained from records in the central office). Age of residents was broken down as follows: 18–44, 45–64, 65–74, 75 and over. (For a detailed discussion of how homes were assigned to age strata in cases in which there were residents of different ages, see Sherman, Newman, and Frenkel 1982.) All 39 homes associated with the urban site were used. Then 61 homes were selected at random from the 122 associated with the rural site in order to complete the cells in each age stratum, that is, in order to have 25 homes representing each of the four age groupings. A 20 percent oversample of homes was also selected by the same method to provide for replacements in the event that some of the interviews planned for the study could not be conducted. Once all the homes were categorized according to the four age strata, residents to be interviewed were randomly selected from among those residents in the designated age range in each home. In addition to one resident from each home, the care providers from the homes were interviewed to provide data on themselves and the homes and further information on the selected residents.

Twenty-three residents from the original sample, fairly evenly distributed across the age groupings, were excluded from the second study. Of the 23, 9 were determined to be ineligible (5 returned to the hospital, and 4 had been discharged or were for other reasons no longer in the home), leaving only 91 eligible in the original sample. The other 14 were excluded because 9 were considered to be too confused, disturbed, or hostile, and 5 were non-English speakers. Eighteen new residents were selected from the oversample to replace those who had been excluded. An inspection of the reasons for exclusion indicated that the remaining study sample might be unduly biased toward those residents who had a greater potential for community integration. In order to remedy this situation in part and to obtain a more accurate view of the community integration of the entire population, data were obtained from care providers on an additional 6 residents who had been included in the original sample but who could not actually be interviewed. Therefore, 95 residents and 101 care providers were interviewed to construct the final sample. Since 18 needed to be added to the sample of 91 eligibles, for a total of 109 attempts, the response rate for the 95 residents was 87 percent, and for the 101 providers it was 93 percent.

In the third study (OMR), conducted in 1982, a stratified random sample of 151 family care residents was drawn through a two-step procedure. The staff of the New York State OMR provided a computer-generated list of 3 clients (selected at random) in each of the counties of New York State having family care homes. The list was stratified so that half of the total group of clients were aged 45–60 and the other half were over 60 years of age. Since this list included in some cases more than 1 client from a single home, and the design called for only 1 client per home, the sample was completed by selecting at random from additional lists provided by the regional family care coordinators of all family care residents aged

45 or older. In order to obtain 150 interviews, attempts were made to interview 161 providers. We exceeded our goal and interviewed 151, with a resulting response rate of 94 percent. Reasons for non-response on the part of the provider were as follows: 4 refused, 2 were out of town, 2 did not understand the questions, 1 was deaf, and 1 was in the hospital. The selection procedures resulted in a range of 0 to 6 homes per county, with the mode being 2 homes per county.

It should be kept in mind that the sampling was done differently in all three studies, and only the third study attempted to be representative of the entire state. In the first two studies samples were selected from particular catchment areas, so we should be cautious about generalization.

Appendix 3 · Factor Analysis of Familism Items

In study 1 a factor analysis was performed on sixteen items considered *a priori* to reflect familism. These were divided into four subscales of affection, social interaction, social distance, and ritual.

Three factors emerged with eigenvalues greater than 1.0 (a fourth had an eigenvalue of .97). The two items pertaining to residents playing cards and games with each other and to care providers playing cards and games with them formed a scale of their own (loadings .98 and .58 respectively, eigenvalue 1.44 percent variance = 18.2) and probably reflected an activity dimension rather than a familism dimension. The item pertaining to residents exchanging gifts among themselves loaded evenly on all factors and had no loading greater than .40, probably indicating that the response had more to do with the ability to buy gifts than with familism, so it was dropped. The factor analysis was repeated with only the remaining thirteen items.

The results of the second factor analysis were similar to the first. Three factors with eigenvalues greater than 1.0 emerged. The most clear-cut was factor 3, tapping social distance. The items included shared space in the home, kitchen privileges, and shared meals. If we include factor loadings greater than .50, factor 1 included three of the items from our original grouping of affection: the care provider's relationship with residents, the care provider's perception of the relationship among residents, and the care provider's friendships with residents. Factor 2, composed of three items pertaining to relationships among residents, included one social interaction item, one ritual item, and one affection item. All three of these items could be asked only in the 85 homes with more than one client.

References

Aanes, D. and M. Moen. 1976. Adaptive behavior changes of group home residents. *Mental Retardation* 14:36–40. Cited in Janicki (1981).

Adams, M. 1975. Foster family care for the intellectually disadvantaged child: The current state of practice and some research perspectives. In M. J. Begab and S. A. Richardson, eds., *The Mentally Retarded and Society· A Social Science Perspective*. Baltimore: University Park Press.

Aptekar, H. H. 1965. Foster and home care for adults. In: H. L. Lurie, ed., *Encyclopedia of Social Work*. New York: National Association of Social Workers.

Aviram, V. and S. Segal. 1973. Exclusion of the mentally ill: Reflection of an old problem in a new context. *Archives of General Psychiatry* 29:126–133.

Bachrach. L. 1976. *Deinstitutionalization: An Analytical Review and So-ciological Perspective*. National Institute of Mental Health. USDHEW Publication No. (ADM) 76–351, Superintendent of Documents, GPO, Washington, DC 20402.

Bachrach, L. 1981. A conceptual approach to deinstitutionalization of the mentally retarded: A perspective from the experience of the mentally ill. In R. H. Bruininks et al., eds., *Deinstitutionalization and Commu-nity Adjustment of Mentally Retarded People*.

Baker, B. L., G. B. Seltzer, and M. M. Seltzer. 1974. *As Close as Pos-sible: Community Residences for Retarded Adults*. Boston: Little, Brown.

Bardo, J. W. 1976. Dimensions of community satisfaction in a British new town. *Multivariate Experimental Clinical Research* 2:129–34.

Bengtson, V., L. Burton, and D. Mangen. 1981. Family support systems and attribution of responsibility: Contrasts among elderly blacks, Mexican-Americans, and whites. Paper presented at the 1981 meetings of the Gerontological Society of America and the Canadian Association of Gerontology, November 10, Toronto, Canada.

Bercovici, S. 1981. Qualitative methods and cultural perspectives in the study of deinstitutionalization. In R. H. Bruininks et al., eds., *Deinstitutionalization and Community Adjustment of Mentally Retarded People.*

Betts, J., S. L. Moore, and P. Reynolds. 1981. A checklist for selecting board-and-care homes for chronic patients. *Hospital and Community Psychiatry* 32:498–500.

Binstock, R. H. 1985. The oldest old: A fresh perspective or compassionate ageism revisited? *Milbank Memorial Fund Quarterly/Health and Society* 63:420–51.

Bjaanes, A. T. and E. W. Butler. 1974. Environmental variation in community care facilities for mentally retarded persons. *American Journal of Mental Deficiency* 78:429–39. Cited in Janicki (1981).

Blackie, N., J. Edelstein, P. S. Matthews, and R. Timmons. 1983. *Alternative Housing and Living Arrangements for Independent Living.* Ann Arbor: National Policy Center on Housing and Living Arrangements for Older Americans, University of Michigan.

Bogen, H. April 20, 1977. Director, Division of Foster Homes for Adults, New York City Human Resources Administration. Personal communication.

Bogen, H. 1979. The history of adult foster home care. In K. H. Nash and D. J. Tesiny, eds., *Readings in Adult Foster Care.* Continuing Education Project, School of Social Welfare, State University of New York at Albany.

Bowlby, J. 1969. *Attachment.* Vol. 1 of *Attachment and Loss.* New York: Basic Books.

Bradshaw, B., W. Vondehaar, V. Kenney, R. S. Tyler, and S. Harris. 1975. Community based residential care for the minimally impaired elderly: A survey analysis. Paper presented at the meeting of the American Geriatrics Society, Miami, Florida.

Braun, K. L. and C. L. Rose. 1986. The Hawaii geriatric foster care experiment: Impact evaluation and cost analysis. *The Gerontologist* 26:516–24.

Brearly, P. C. 1977. *Residential Work with the Elderly.* London: Routledge and Kegan Paul.

Brockett, R. G. 1984. Issues in promoting adult foster care as an option to institutionalization. *Journal of Housing for the Elderly* 2:51–63.

Brody, E. M. 1977. Aging. In J. B. Turner, ed., *Encyclopedia of Social Work*, vol. 1. Washington, D.C.: National Association of Social Workers.

Brody, E. M. 1981. "Women in the middle" and family help to older people. *The Gerontologist* 21:471–80.

Bronfenbrenner, U. 1979. *The Ecology of Human Development: Experi-*

ments by Nature and Design. Cambridge: Harvard University Press.

Browder, J. A., L. Ellis, and J. Neal. 1974. Foster homes: Alternatives to institutions? *Mental Retardation* 12:33–36.

Bruininks, R. H., B. K. Hill, and M. S. Thorsheim. 1980. *A Profile of Foster Home Services for Mentally Retarded Persons in 1977.* Minneapolis: Department of Psychoeducational Studies, University of Minnesota.

Bruininks, R. H., B. K. Hill, and M. J. Thorsheim. 1982. Deinstitutionalization and foster care for mentally retarded people. *Health and Social Work* 7:198–205.

Bruininks, R. H., C. E. Meyers, B. B. Sigford, and K. C. Lakin, eds. 1981. *Deinstitutionalization and Community Adjustment of Mentally Retarded People.* Washington, D.C.: American Association of Mental Deficiency.

Butler, R. N. 1969. Age-ism: Another form of bigotry. *The Gerontologist* 9:243–46.

Carling, P. J., ed. October 1984. *Developing Family Foster Care Programs in Mental Health: A Resource Guide.* Proceedings of the National Institute of Mental Health Workshop on Family Foster Care for "Chronically Mentally Ill" Persons, Rockville, Maryland, March 27–28, 1984. Rockville: Department of Health and Human Services, Public Health Service, Alcohol, Drug Abuse, and Mental Health Administration.

Cocozza, J. J. and H. J. Steadman. 1976. Community fear of the mentally ill: An unsolved obstacle for the community mental health movement. Paper presented at the Conference on Community and Policy Research, State University of New York at Albany, April 30.

Cohen, H. J. and D. Kligler, eds. 1980. *Urban Community Care for the Developmentally Disabled.* Springfield, Il: Charles C. Thomas.

Collins, A. H. and D. L. Pancoast. Undated. *Natural Helping Networks: A Strategy for Prevention.* Washington, D.C.: National Association of Social Workers.

Cotten, P. D., G. F. P. Sison, and S. Starr. 1981. Comparing elderly retarded and non-retarded individuals: Who are they? What are their needs? *The Gerontologist* 21:359–65.

Crockett, H. M. 1934. Boarding homes as a tool in social casework with mental patients. *Mental Hygiene* 18:189–204.

Crutcher, H. B. 1944. *Foster Home Care for Mental Patients.* New York: Commonwealth Fund.

Cumming, J. 1968. Screening of admissions. Memorandum 68–27, Division of Mental Health, New York State Department of Mental Hygiene, Albany.

Dale, N. J. May 1980. Evaluation of the Medicaid Foster Family Care Pilot Project. Massachusetts Department of Public Welfare, Office of Research and Evaluation, mimeographed.

David, T. G., R. H. Moos, and J. R. Kahn. 1981. Community integration among elderly residents of sheltered care settings. *American Journal of Community Psychiatry* 9:513–26.

Davies, S. P. and K. G. Ecob. 1959. *The Mentally Retarded in Society*. New York: Columbia University Press.

DiGiovanni, L. 1978. The elderly retarded: A little-known group. *The Gerontologist* 18: 262–66.

Epple, W. 1982. Personal communication to J. W. Jacobson, Program Research Unit, New York State Office of Mental Retardation and Developmental Disabilities, Albany, New York.

Estes, C. L. 1979. *The Aging Enterprise*. San Francisco: Jossey-Bass.

Follett, S. 1977. Protective services for adults. In J. B. Turner, ed., *Encyclopedia of Social Work*, vol. 2. Washington, D.C.: National Association of Social Workers.

Furukawa, C. and D. Shomaker. 1982. *Community Health Services for the Aged*. Rockville, Md.: Aspen Systems.

Giovannoni, J. M. and L. Ullmann. 1961. Characteristics of family care homes. *International Journal of Social Psychiatry* 7:299–306.

Goffman, E. 1961. *Asylums*. New York: Anchor Books.

Gollay, E. 1976. *A Study of the Community Adjustment of Deinstitutionalized Mentally Retarded Persons*. Vol. 5: *An Analysis of Factors Associated with Community Adjustment* (Contract No. OEC–0–74–9183). Cambridge, Mass.: U.S. Office of Education.

Hammerman, J., H. H. Friedsam, and H. Shore. 1975. Management perspectives in long-term care facilities. In S. Sherwood, ed., *Long-Term Care*.

Handy, I. A. 1968. Foster care as a therapeutic program for geriatric psychiatric patients. *Journal of the American Geriatrics Society* 16:350–58.

Hauber, F. A., R. H. Bruininks, B. K. Hill, K. C. Lakin, and C. C. White. 1982. *National Census of Residential Facilities: Fiscal Year 1982*. Minneapolis: University of Minnesota, Department of Educational Psychology.

Herz, K. 1971. Community resources and services to help independent living. *The Gerontologist* 11:59–66.

Hill, B. K., R. H. Bruininks, K. C. Lakin, F. A. Hauber, and S. P. McGuire. 1984. *Stability of Mental Retardation Facilities for Mentally Retarded People: 1977–1982 (Brief No. 22)*. Minneapolis: Center for Residential and Community Services, University of Minnesota, Department of Educational Psychology.

Hill, B. K. and K. C. Lakin. 1984. *Trends in Residential Services for Mentally Retarded People: 1977–1982 (Brief No. 23)*. Minneapolis: Center for Residential and Community Services, University of Minnesota, Department of Educational Psychology.

Hochschild, A. R. 1973. *The Unexpected Community*. Englewood Cliffs, N.J.: Prentice-Hall.

Horizon House Institute for Research and Development. 1975. *Community*

Careers: The Assessment of the Life Adjustment of Former Mental Hospital Patients. 1019 Stafford House, 5555 Wissahickon Avenue, Philadelphia, PA 19144.

Hull, J. T. and J. C. Thompson. 1981a. Factors contributing to normalization in residential facilities for mentally retarded persons. *Mental Retardation,* 19:69–73.

Hull, J. T. and J. C. Thompson. 1981b. Factors which contribute to normalization in residential facilities for the mentally ill. *Community Mental Health Journal* 7:107–13.

Intagliata, J., N. Crosby, and L. Neider. 1981. Foster family care for mentally retarded people: A qualitative review. In R. H. Bruininks et al., eds., *Deinstitutionalization and Community Adjustment of Mentally Retarded People.*

Intagliata, J. and B. Willer. 1981. A review of training programs for providers of foster family care to mentally retarded persons. In R. H. Bruininks et al., eds., *Deinstitutionalization and Community Adjustment of Mentally Retarded People.*

Intagliata, J., B. Willer, and N. Wicks. 1981. Factors related to the quality of community adjustment in family care homes. In R. H. Bruininks et al., eds., *Deinstitutionalization and Community Adjustment of Mentally Retarded People.*

Jacobson, J. W., A. A. Schwartz, and M. P. Janicki. 1984. Rehabilitative models and residential programme services. In R. I. Brown, ed., *Integrated Programmes for Handicapped Adolescents and Adults.* London: Croom Helm. New York: Nichols.

Janicki, M. P. 1981. Personal growth and community residence environments: A review. In H. C. Haywood and J. R. Newbrough, eds., *Living Environments for Developmentally Retarded Persons.* Baltimore: University Park Press.

Janicki, M. P. and J. W. Jacobson. 1984. Health and support services for mentally retarded elders living in foster care and group homes. Paper presented as part of symposium, "Community Living: The Environment of Elderly Retarded Persons," at the 37th annual meeting of the Gerontological Society of America, San Antonio, Texas, November 20.

Janicki, M. P. and A. E. MacEachron. 1984. Residential, health, and social service need patterns of elderly developmentally disabled persons. *The Gerontologist* 24:128–37.

Janicki, M. P. and H. Wisniewski, eds. 1985. *Aging and Developmental Disabilities: Issues and Approaches.* Baltimore: Brookes.

Jansen, L. T. 1952. Measuring family solidarity. *American Sociological Review* 17:727–33.

Justice, R. S., J. Bradley, and G. O'Connor. 1971. Foster family care for the retarded: Management concerns for the caretaker. *Mental Retardation* 9 (4):12–15.

Kahana, E. 1982. A congruence model of person-environment interaction.

198 · References

In M. P. Lawton, P. G. Windley, and T. O. Byerts, eds., *Aging and the Environment: Theoretical Approaches.* New York: Springer.

Kahana, E. and R. M. Coe. 1975. Alternatives in long-term care. In S. Sherwood, ed., *Long-Term Care.*

Kingson, E. R., B. A. Hirshorn, and J. M. Cornman. 1986. *Ties That Bind: The Interdependence of Generations (A Report from the Gerontological Society of America).* Washington, D.C.: Seven Locks Press.

Kirk, S. A. and M. E. Therrien. 1975. Community mental health myths and the fate of former hospitalized patients. *Psychiatry* 38:209–17.

Klapp, O. E. 1959–60. Ritual and family solidarity. *Social Forces* 37: 212–14.

Kramer, M. 1970. Problems in psychiatric epidemiology. *Proceedings of the Royal Society of Medicine* 63:553–62.

Kramer, M., C. A. Taube, and R. W. Redick. 1973. Patterns of use of psychiatric facilities by the aged: Past, present, and future. In C. Eisdorfer and M. P. Lawton, eds., *The Psychology of Adult Development and Aging.* Washington, D.C.: American Psychological Association.

Krauss, M. W. and M. M. Seltzer. 1986. National survey of programs serving elderly mentally retarded persons: A summary report of findings. Starr Center for Mental Retardation at Brandeis University, Eunice Kennedy Shriver Center, and School of Social Work at Boston University.

Kultgen, P. B. and R. W. Habenstein. 1981. Dynamics of support for deinstitutionalized elderly mental patients in selected catchment areas in Missouri. University of Missouri, Columbia.

Lamb, H. R. and V. Goertzel. 1971. Discharged mental patients—are they really in the community? *Archives of General Psychiatry* 24:29–34.

Lauber, D. and F. S. Bangs. 1974. *Zoning for Family Group Care Facilities (Planning Advisory Service Report No. 300).* Chicago: American Society of Planning Officials.

Lawton, M. P. 1970. Ecology and aging. In L. A. Pastalan and D. H. Carson, eds., *The Spatial Behavior of Older People.* Ann Arbor: Institute of Gerontology, University of Michigan.

Lawton, M. P. 1982. Competence, environmental press, and the adaptation of older people. In M. P. Lawton, P. G. Windley, and T. O. Byerts, eds., *Aging and the Environment: Theoretical Approaches.* New York: Springer.

Lawton, M. P. 1984. Discussant comments at symposium on "Community Living: The Environment of Elderly Retarded Persons," 37th annual meeting of the Gerontological Society of America, San Antonio, Texas, November 20.

Lawton, M. P. and J. Bader. 1970. Wish for privacy by young and old. *Journal of Gerontology* 25:48–54.

Lawton, M. P., M. Greenbaum, and B. Liebowitz. 1980. The lifespan of housing environments for the aging. *The Gerontologist* 20:56–64.

Lawton, M. P. and C. Hoffman. 1984. Neighborhood reactions to elderly housing. *Journal of Housing for the Elderly* 2:41–53.

Lawton, M. P., M. Moss, and M. Grimes. 1985. The changing service needs of older tenants in planned housing. *The Gerontologist* 25:258–64.

Lawton, M. P. and L. Nahemow. 1973. Ecology and the aging process. In C. Eisdorfer and M. P. Lawton, eds., *The Psychology of Adult Development and Aging*. Washington, D.C.: American Psychological Association.

Lawton, M. P. and B. Simon. 1968. The ecology of social relationships in housing for the elderly. *The Gerontologist* 8:108–15.

Lin, A. January 9, 1987. Associate commissioner, Program Design and Services, New York State Office of Mental Retardation and Developmental Disabilities, Albany. Personal communication.

Linn, M. W. 1981. Can foster care survive? In R. Budson, ed., *New Directions for Mental Health Services: Issues in Community Residential Care*. San Francisco: Jossey-Bass.

Linn, M. W. and E. M. Caffey, Jr. 1977. Foster placement for the older psychiatric patient. *Journal of Gerontology* 32:340–45.

Linn, M. W., C. J. Klett, and E. M. Caffey, Jr. 1980. Foster home characteristics and psychiatric patient outcome. *Archives of General Psychiatry* 37:129–32.

Lowy, L. 1980. *Social Policies and Programs for the Aged*. Lexington, Mass.: D. C. Heath.

Maddox, G. L. 1975. Families as context and resource in chronic illness. In S. Sherwood, ed., *Long-Term Care*.

Maletz, L. 1942. Family care—a method of rehabilitation. *Mental Hygiene* 26:594–605.

Mangum, W. P. 1985a. But not in my neighborhood: Community resistance to housing for the elderly. *Journal of Housing for the Elderly* 3:101–19.

Mangum, W. P. 1985b. Community receptivity to housing for the elderly as a type of group housing. Unpublished Manuscript, University of South Florida.

Markson, E. W. 1985. After deinstitutionalization, what? *Journal of Geriatric Psychiatry* 18:37–56.

McCoin, J. M. 1983. *Adult Foster Homes: Their Managers and Residents*. New York: Human Sciences Press.

McNeel, B. H. 1965. Family care. *American Journal of Psychiatry* 121: 701–3.

Miller, M. C. 1977. A program for adult foster care. *Social Work* 22: 275–79.

Moos, R. H. 1977. Evaluating sheltered care settings for the elderly. Paper presented at the VA/NASA Conference on Habitability in Extended

Care Environments, Minneapolis, September.

Moos, R. H. and S. Lemke. 1979. Multiphasic environmental assessment procedure: Sheltered Care Project. Social Ecology Laboratory, VA Medical Center and Stanford University School of Medicine, Palo Alto, California.

Mor, V., S. Sherwood, and C. Gutkin. 1986. A national study of residential care for the aged. *The Gerontologist* 26:405–17.

Morrissey, J. P. 1982. Deinstitutionalizing the mentally ill: Process, outcomes, and new directions. In W. R. Gore, ed., *Deviance and Mental Illness*. Beverly Hills, Calif.: Sage.

Morrissey, J. R. 1965. Family care for the mentally ill: A neglected therapeutic resource. *Social Service Review* 39:63–71.

Morrissey, J. R. 1966. Status of family care programs. *Mental Retardation* 4 (5):8–11.

Morrissey, J. R. 1967. The case for family care of the mentally ill. *Community Mental Health Journal Monograph No. 2*. New York: Behavioral Publications.

Murphy, H. B. M., B. Pennee, and D. Luchins. 1972. Foster homes: The new back wards? *Canada's Mental Health*, supplement no. 71, September–October.

Newman, E. S., D. J. Newman, and M. L. Gewirtz, eds. 1984. *Elderly Criminals*. Boston: Oelgeschlager, Gunn and Hain.

O'Connor, G. 1976. *Home Is a Good Place: A National Perspective of Community Residential Facilities for Developmentally Disabled Persons (Monograph No. 2)*. Washington, D.C.: American Association of Mental Deficiency.

Oktay, J. S. 1987. Foster care for adults. In *Encyclopedia of Social Work*, 18th ed., Silver Spring, Md.: National Association of Social Workers.

Oktay, J. S. and P. J. Volland. 1981. Community care program for the elderly. *Health and Social Work* 6:41–47.

Oriol, W. E. 1980. *Housing the Elderly Deinstitutionalized Mental Hospital Patient in the Community*. Washington, D.C.: International Center for Social Gerontology.

Parigot, J. 1863. The Gheel question from an American point of view. *American Journal of Insanity* 19:332–54.

Pfeiffer, E., ed. 1973. *Alternatives to Institutional Care for Older Americans: Practice and Planning*. Durham, N.C.: Duke University.

Plummer, C. June 9, 1986. Deputy commissioner, Division of Adult Services, New York State Department of Social Services. Letter to commissioners of local social services districts, Albany.

Pollock, H. M. 1945. A brief history of family care of mental patients in America. *American Journal of Psychiatry* 102:351–61.

Provencal, G. and J. P. MacCormack. October 1979. Adult foster care: Paradox and possibility. *Polestar*, 1:4.

Pumphrey, R. E. 1965. Social welfare in the United States. In H. L. Lurie, ed., *Encyclopedia of Social Work*. New York: National Association of Social Workers.

Rabbitt, W. J. January 1987. Director, Adult Community Services, Division of Adult Services, New York State Department of Social Services, Albany. Personal communication.

Redding, R. A. 1963. The importance of early family experience in placement of psychotic patients. *Social Work* 8:72–76.

Rejino, E. January 23, 1987. Statewide Family Care coordinator, New York State Office of Mental Health, Albany. Personal communication.

Richmond, C. 1971. Therapeutic housing. In H. R. Lamb and Associates, *Rehabilitation in Community Mental Health*. Washington, D.C. Jossey-Bass.

Risdorfer, E. N., G. Primanis, and L. Doretz. 1971. Family care as a useful alternative to the long-term hospital confinement of geropsychiatric patients. *Journal of American Geriatrics Society* 19:150–58.

Rose, T., M. P. Janicki, and E. Ansello. 1986–87. Aging and developmental disabilities. *AGHE Exchange*, vol. 10, no. 2. Washington, D.C.: Association for Gerontology in Higher Education.

Sable, P. 1979. Differentiating between attachment and dependency in theory and practice. *Social Casework* 60:138–44.

Sainer, J. S., S. Ochs, M. Levendos, and D. Moorhus. 1977. Components of a community based program for the frail elderly. Paper presented at the 30th annual meeting of the Gerontological Society, San Francisco, November.

Savasta, J. A. 1979. The aged mental patient: A return to the community. Paper presented at the annual meeting of the Gerontological Society, Washington, D.C.

Schulberg, H. C., A. Becker, and M. McGrath. 1976. Planning the phase down of mental hospitals. *Community Mental Health* 12:3–12.

Segal, S. P. and U. Aviram. 1978. *The Mentally Ill in Community Based Sheltered Care: A Study of Community Care and Social Integration*. New York: Wiley Interscience.

Segal, S. P. and J. Baumohl. 1983. Deinstitutionalization. In *Encyclopedia of Social Work*. 17th ed. supplement. Silver Spring, Md.: National Association of Social Workers.

Segal, S. P., J. Baumohl, and E. W. Moyles. 1980. Neighborhood types and community reaction to the mentally ill: A paradox of intensity. *Journal of Health and Social Behavior* 21:345–59.

Seltzer, M. M., G. B. Seltzer, and C. C. Sherwood. 1982. Comparison of community adjustment of older vs. younger mentally retarded adults. *American Journal of Mental Deficiencies* 87:9–13.

Sherman, S. R. 1979. The retirement housing setting: Site permeability, service availability, and perceived community support in crises. *Journal of Social Service Research* 3:139–57.

Sherman, S. R. 1985. Housing. In A. Monk, ed., *Handbook of Geron-*

tological Services. New York: Van Nostrand Reinhold.

Sherman, S. R., E. R. Frenkel, and E. S. Newman. 1986. Community participation of mentally ill adults in foster family care. *Journal of Community Psychology* 14:120–33.

Sherman, S. R. and E. S. Newman. 1976. Options in intermediate sheltered housing for the elderly. Institute of Gerontology, State University of New York at Albany. Mimeo.

Sherman, S. R. and E. S. Newman. 1977. Foster-family care for the elderly in New York State. *The Gerontologist* 17:513–20.

Sherman, S. R. and E. S. Newman. 1979. The role of the caseworker in adult foster care. *Social Work* 24:324–28.

Sherman, S. R., E. S. Newman, and E. R. Frenkel. 1982. Community integration of mentally ill adults in (foster) family care. Final report to New York State Health Research Council. State University of New York at Albany. Mimeo.

Sherman, S. R., E. S. Newman, and L. Kucij. 1981. Career development in mental health care for the aged: An integrated training model for the professional and non-professional. *Gerontology and Geriatrics Education* 2:133–37.

Sherman, S. R. and D. A. Snider. 1981. Social participation in adult homes: Deinstitutionalized mental patients and the frail elderly. *The Gerontologist* 21:545–50.

Sherwood, S. 1977. Institutions for adults. In J. B. Turner, ed., *Encyclopedia of Social Work,* vol. 1. Washington, D.C. National Association of Social Workers.

Sherwood, S., ed. 1975. *Long-Term Care: A Handbook for Researchers, Planners, and Providers.* New York: Spectrum Publications.

Sherwood, S. and J. N. Morris. 1983. The Pennsylvania domiciliary care experiment: I. Impact on quality of life. *American Journal of Public Health* 73:646–53.

State of New York. BSW (Board of Social Welfare). Undated. *Rules: Family-type Proprietary Homes for Adults.* Albany.

State of New York. DMH (Department of Mental Hygiene). 1974. *Department Policy Manual.* Albany.

State of New York. DMH. 1976. *Manual for Family Care Providers.* Albany.

State of New York. DSS (Department of Social Services). 1971. *Report on Family-type Private Proprietary Homes for Adults.* Albany.

State of New York. DSS. March 1973. *Foster Family Care for Adults Program, Bulletin 188.* Albany.

State of New York. DSS. April 24, 1984. *Proposed Regulation Section 486.7(d) and part 489.* Albany.

State of New York. DSS. August 16, 1985. *Administrative Directive, 85 ADM–36 (Adult Services).* Albany.

State of New York. DSS. November 15, 1985. *Administrative Directive, 85 ADM-46 (Adult Services)*. Albany.

State of New York OMH (Office of Mental Health). March 1, 1983. *Annual Report on Community Living Programs*. Albany.

State of New York. OMH. 1985. *1984 Level of Care Survey*. Albany.

State of New York. OMH. October 1, 1986. *1987 Update and Progress Report for the Five Year Comprehensive Plan for Mental Health Services, 1985–1990*. Albany.

State of New York. OMR (Office of Mental Retardation and Developmental Disabilities). 1980. *Comprehensive Plan for Services to Mentally Retarded and Developmentally Disabled Persons, 1981–1984*. Albany.

State of New York. OMR. November 1983. *Report of the Committee on Aging and Developmental Disabilities*. Albany.

State of New York. OMR. July 1986. *Family Care Policy Manual*. B/DDSO ed. Albany.

State of New York. OMR. Undated. *Community Living for the Mentally Retarded and Developmentally Disabled*. Albany.

Steinhauer, M. B. 1982. Geriatric foster care: A prototype design and implementation issues. *The Gerontologist* 22:293–300.

Streib, G. F. 1978. An alternative family form for older persons: Need and social context. *The Family Coordinator* 27:413–20.

Stroud, M. and M. Murphy. November 1984. *The Aged Mentally Retarded/Developmentally Disabled in Northeast Ohio, 1982*. Akron, Ohio: University of Akron.

Stycos, J. M. 1951. Family care—a neglected area of research. *Psychiatry* 14:301–6.

Taietz, P. 1964. The extended family in transition: A study of the family life of old people in the Netherlands. *Sociologia Ruralis* 4:63–74.

Talmadge, H. and D. F. Murphy. February 1983. Innovative home care program offers appropriate alternative for elderly. *Hospital Progress* 64:50–51, 72.

Tesiny, E. January 1987. Research scientist, New York State Office of Mental Retardation and Developmental Disabilities, Albany. Personal communication.

Tinsley, D. J., G. O'Connor, and A. S. Halpern. 1973. *The Identification of Problem Areas in the Establishment and Maintenance of Community Residential Facilities for the Developmentally Disabled (Working Paper No. 64)*. Eugene, Oreg.: Rehabilitation and Training Center on Mental Retardation.

Titmuss, R. M. 1968. *Commitment in Welfare*. New York: Pantheon Books. Cited in McCoin (1983.)

Tobin, S. S. 1975. Social and health services for the future aged. *The Gerontologist* Vol. 15, part 2, pp. 32–37.

Touissaint, J. and P. Butler. 1967. Placement of suitable psychogeriatric patients in boarding houses. *Medical Journal of Australia* 1:904–6.

United States Department of Health, Education, and Welfare. August 1964. *Aging*, no. 118, pp. 1–3, 16.

Vandivort, R., G. M. Kurren, and K. Braun. 1984. Foster family care for frail elderly: A cost-effective quality care alternative. *Journal of Gerontological Social Work* 7:101–14.

Veteran's Administration. 1975. *Field Station Summary*, vol. 18, no. 2. Washington, D.C.

Walz, T., D. Harper, and J. Wilson. 1986. The aging developmentally disabled person: A review. *The Gerontologist* 26:622–29.

Watt, N. F. 1970. Five-year follow-up of geriatric chronically ill mental patients in foster home care. *Journal of American Geriatrics Society* 18:310–16.

Wehmeyer, B. October 1981. Family care: Giving someone the challenge to come home. *This Month in Mental Health*. Albany: New York State Office of Mental Health.

Willer, B. and J. Intagliata. 1984. *Promises and Realities for Mentally Retarded Citizens: Life in the Community*. Baltimore: University Park Press.

Wolpert, J., M. Dear, and R. Crawford. 1975. Satellite mental health facilities. *Ekistics* 40:342–47.

Zelizer, V. A. 1985. *Pricing the Priceless Child: The Changing Social Value of Children*. New York: Basic Books.

Other Publications Reporting Individual Studies

Newman, E. S. and S. R. Sherman. 1977. A survey of caretakers in adult foster homes. *The Gerontologist* 17:436–39.

Newman, E. S. and S. R. Sherman. 1979a. Community integration of the elderly in foster family care. *Journal of Gerontological Social Work* 1:175–86.

Newman, E. S. and S. R. Sherman. 1979b. Foster-family care for the elderly: Surrogate family or mini-institution? *International Journal of Aging and Human Development* 10:165–76.

Newman, E. S., S. R. Sherman, and E. F. Frenkel. 1985. Foster family care: A residential alternative for mentally retarded older persons. In M. P. Janicki and H. Wisniewski, eds., *Aging and Developmental Disabilities: Issues and Approaches*. Baltimore: Brookes.

Sherman, S. R., E. R. Frenkel, and E. S. Newman. 1984. Foster family care for older persons who are mentally retarded. *Mental Retardation* 22:302–8.

Sherman, S. R., E. S. Newman, and E. R. Frenkel. 1984. Community acceptance of mentally ill adults in (foster) family care. *Health and Social Work* 9:188–99.

Author Index

Subject Index